ANSWERS BOOK 4 TEENS

VOL 2

W9-AWN-160

Master Books®

First printing: July 2012
Second printing: January 2013

Master Books®, P.O. Box 726, Green Forest, AR 72638
Master Books® is a division of the New Leaf Publishing Group, Inc.

ISBN: 978-0-89051-660-7
Library of Congress Number: 2011937097

Cover and Interior Layout by Justin Skinner

Unless otherwise noted, Scripture quotations are from the New King James Version of the Bible.

Please consider requesting that a copy of this volume be purchased by your local library system.

Printed in China

Please visit our website for other great titles: www.masterbooks.net

For information regarding author interviews, please contact the publicity department at (870) 438-5288

Master
Books®
A Division of New Leaf Publishing Group
www.masterbooks.net

Contents

Acknowledgments

Many thanks to those who reviewed and edited portions of this book: Dr. Tommy Mitchell, Roger Patterson, Dr. Andrew Snelling, Ken Ham, Tim Chaffey, Troy Lacey, Dr. Elizabeth Mitchell, Paul Taylor, Frost Smith, David Wright, Steve Golden, and Bodie Hodge.

Introduction

As any teen probably knows, school can be a great place and a terrible place — whether public/state schools, Christian schools, or even home schools! In public schools and in some Christian schools, things can sometimes get even worse for Christians, especially when false information and false claims about the Bible are often repeated. Sometimes teachers and sometimes students make these false claims — and many times they do not realize the errors of these claims.

But I want to encourage you as Christians to be discerning on these issues. I understand some of you who are reading this may not be Christians or may be unsure of what you believe, so let me take this time to encourage you to consider the claims of the Bible and of Jesus Christ. We invite you to receive Christ as Lord. To understand this more, please read the last chapter of this book, which explains this good news of how you can be saved and go to heaven.

Discernment means to have understanding and wisdom about issues so you can see what is right and what is wrong. For example, if someone said, "God exists, but He is evil," the discerning person would recognize that the person claiming this is both right…and wrong. This statement is right because God does exist. But it is wrong in saying that God is evil. The Bible says:

Test all things; hold fast what is good (1 Thessalonians 5:21).

Let's look at some false claims and misconceptions so that you can learn to be discerning if they pop up in discussions with teachers, other students, or even your parents!

Spotting False Claims and Misconceptions

Here are some false claims and some brief responses:

1. **The Bible teaches that the earth is flat.** Of course, this is nowhere in Scripture and the Bible informs us that the earth is round (e.g., Isaiah 40:22, "the circle of the earth," or Job 26:10, with "a circular horizon").

   Instead, this flat earth idea was a false Greek mythology (~500 B.C.) that, sadly, a few Christians actually bought into around A.D. 300. And it was fellow Christians who had to refute this idea, using the Bible. People who attack the Bible actually pull verses out of context to try to say it teaches that the earth is flat. One of these verses is Revelation 7:1, which in prophetic language refers to the "four corners of the earth." But this is clearly a metaphor for the four directions (north, south, east, and west). If we're using discernment when we read, we see that it obviously does not imply a flat earth.

2. **Creationists don't believe animals change.** This false claim is set up to try to make Christians look ignorant. Usually, the critics will say, "Evolution means animals change, but creationists don't believe animals change. Since we see animals change every day, evolution is true and the creationists are wrong!"

   But creationists do believe animals change. Even in the Bible, Jacob did selective breeding to make animal changes happen quickly (Genesis 30:31–43). So changes in animals are not a problem for creationists. The difference between evolutionists and creationists is the AMOUNT of change. This is the part that requires discernment.

The evolutionist says that change in animals is huge, like an amoeba changing into a goat over millions of years. But we don't observe this, do we? In fact, no one can observe this over millions of years. Creationists, however, say there is change within a respective kind *(versus a species, which has a definition that changes a lot)*. What do we mean by "kind"? We explain it in detail in chapter 2 of this book.

3. **Creationists don't believe in science.** Those who level this claim at Christians often say that it's "religion versus science."

But what they fail to realize is that science comes out of a biblical worldview. God upholds the universe in a consistent fashion (Hebrews 1:3; Genesis 8:22); therefore, the laws of nature will be the same tomorrow as they are today, until the end of the world. If everything exploded from nothing, like the big-bang idea teaches, why would we have all these beautiful laws in the universe and why are they upheld so perfectly? This is why we can formulate laws of science and do scientific experiments. Most of the fields of science were developed by Bible-believing creationists like Faraday, Boyle, Mendel, Newton, and many others.

So why do some people say it's "religion versus science"? This is called a "bait and switch" fallacy. They are actually "baiting" you with the good meaning of science, which is the repeatable and observable science that we all do. Their "bait" conjures up in your mind great scientific achievements *(computers, mixing chemicals in a test tube, rockets, jets, and more)*, all of which are repeatable and observable, but then they "switch" the definition out from under you. They switch to a lesser-known definition of science, "naturalistic evolution," which is not repeatable or observable. When people make the claim that it's "religion versus science," they really mean it's "biblical creation versus evolution." And this is really a religion versus a religion.

There is also the issue of origins *(historical)* versus operational science, the highly reliable and repeatable science that has a tremendous reputation. This is the type of science that put men on the moon, builds computers and automobiles, develops genetic mapping, etc. As Christians, we fully believe in operational science. In fact, most of these fields of science were developed by Christians.

The other science is called historical science. It isn't repeatable because it deals with events in the past. Evolution, radiometric dating, etc., deal with reconstructing the past, so it requires quite a few assumptions to fill in the gaps. These assumptions are called "interpretations" and they are not repeatable science.

Many times, these assumptions change and are shown wrong and the whole concept of what was believed changes. This happens frequently in historical science, which is not very reliable and changes quite often. Sometimes I wonder why it is even called "science" with such a bad reputation and non-repeatability. It makes people lose hope in good operational science just because it uses the name "science." Some people even get confused and think the reputation of operational science can be applied to historical science, which it should not.

These are just a few things to be discerning about when people make false claims or present false information. Of course, there are many others, like the number of "species" on the ark *(it should be "kinds")*, mutation and natural selection, or that "the Bible is full of contradictions." These misconceptions are what spurred us on to write this book! We hope to address many of these claims in a way that will answer your questions and help you develop discernment for those times when people approach you with misconceptions about the Bible. In this way, you can be a light to the people around you so that they also can learn to trust that the Bible is true.

Q1 Did creation really take just 6 days or did God use

THE BIG BANG?

Ken Ham

I know you probably don't like taking tests — it sort of feels like being at school! But how about taking a test for me? I assure you, it is a very easy test. Grab your Bible and read through Genesis chapter 1. As you do, look for any hint in Genesis 1 — don't think about what you may have heard! — that God supposedly took millions of years to create the universe, including all the life forms on earth.

While you do this, also look for any suggestion at all that the Bible teaches something like the big-bang idea about the origin of the universe. *(Here's a hint for you: the big-bang idea teaches that the universe began about 13–15 billion years ago, the sun came before the earth, and earth formed after the sun as a hot molten blob that took millions of years to cool down!)* Okay, time's up! What did you find?

WHAT DID YOU LEARN FROM THE TEST?

If you read only the account in Genesis chapter 1, you see that God created space, matter, and time at the beginning. The earth was created as water; it obviously was not a hot molten blob that cooled down for millions of years.

The sun, the moon, and all the stars were not created until the fourth day — after the earth was formed. So it's obvious — the big-bang idea does not fit with the Bible at all! Either the big-bang model is correct and the Bible is wrong; or the Bible is correct and the big–bang model is wrong.

And do you know what? The secularists who propose the big-bang idea were not there to see it happen — they don't have digital photographs of the big bang occurring! However, God, who knows everything and has always been here, had written down in His Word what did happen — and that's the record we read in Genesis 1. Wouldn't you rather believe the trustworthy Witness who knows everything and who was there, instead of the words of finite, sinful humans, whose hearts are against God because of their sin nature, who don't know everything, and who weren't there?

Now as you read Genesis 1, did you get the idea that God took billions of years to create everything? No, you read that God created in six days. For instance, we can read exactly what God created on the first day of creation:

> *Then God said, "Let there be light"; and there was light...God called the light Day, and the darkness He called Night. So the evening and the morning were the first day (Genesis 1:3–5).*

HOW LONG WAS A "DAY"?

Some people ask the question, "But what does the word day mean in Genesis 1? Could it mean a period of millions of years?"

Well, let's go to Hebrew experts. We are going to consult a Hebrew lexicon, which is a Hebrew dictionary. A modern and very scholarly Hebrew lexicon is that produced by Kohler and Baumgartner.[1] When we look up the meaning of the Hebrew word for "day" *(the word yom)*, we find it has a number of different meanings. Why is that?

Well, most words have two or more meanings depending on the context. For instance, the English word day can have different meanings. Consider this sentence:

Back in my father's **day**, it took 10 **days** to drive across the outback during the **day**.

Here, there are three different meanings for the word day:

- Day—meaning time *("father's day")*
- Day—meaning an ordinary day *("10 days")*
- Day—meaning daylight portion of a day *("during the day")*

It is the context that determines the meaning of the word day. This is also true of the Hebrew language. Now when we look up the meaning of the word day in the Hebrew dictionary I mentioned above, we find a range of meanings, but look at the second definition of the word day. The lexicon gives the first example of where day means an ordinary day as in Genesis 1:5 — the first day of the creation week:

Yom: "Day of twenty-four hours: Genesis 1:5"[2]

Now why is it that the authors determined that the meaning of the word day in Genesis 1:5 is an ordinary, approximately 24-hour day? Well, let's look at the context. Whenever the word day (*yom*) is used with a number (*e.g., the first day*), the word evening, the word morning, or the phrase "evening and morning" is used — so the meaning is an ordinary day. That is the contextual usage for each of the six days of creation! Note that the same Hebrew word for "day" (*yom*) is used in Genesis 2:4 and Genesis 3:5, but in those instances it means "time," since yom is not qualified by a number, or "evening" or "morning."

In fact, the Hebrew word for "day" is used 2,301 times in the Old Testament, in the singular and plural forms. It often meant an ordinary day — but it has other meanings depending on the context. For instance, it means "time" when used in the phrases "the day of the Lord" and "the time of the judges."[3]

WHY QUESTION DAY IN GENESIS 1 AND NOWHERE ELSE?

Here's a challenging point for you! Christians know what the word day means everywhere it is used in the Old Testament, except in one place — Genesis chapter 1! Now why is that? It really is because many Christians have been influenced to believe in the idea that the universe is billions of years old, and they try to fit this into the days of creation *(prior to Adam)*.

If these Christian critics were consistent, they should also be arguing that one can fit millions of years into the six days that Joshua marched around Jericho (Joshua 6:3 and 14); or the week that Noah spent loading the animals into the ark before the Flood (Genesis 7:1–4); or perhaps Jonah spent millions of years in a great fish (Jonah 1:17); or maybe Jesus spent millions of years in the grave (Acts 10:40)! Such things are absurd.

To try to justify this, Christian critics often say, "The days couldn't be normal 24-hour days since the sun didn't exist until day 4." But all you need for a normal 24-hour day is a light source and a rotating earth! We had a light source on day 1 (Genesis 1:3) and the sun took over the duties of providing light on the earth on day 4 (Genesis 1:15–16). So this is not a problem.

Sometimes Christian critics try to say that a day is like a thousand years as in 2 Peter 3:8. But if each of the days of creation is a thousand years, that still doesn't add up to billions of years! At most, that would add about 6,000–7,000 extra years. But there is no need to do this since 2 Peter 3:8 is in the context of the Lord's patience, not the days of creation. Besides, 2 Peter 3:8 *(the second part of the verse)* says a thousand years are like day! So there goes that argument!
The point is, why not read the Bible the way it was meant to be read?

In other words, these Christians believe man's fallible ideas about the age of the universe and the earth, and they are reinterpreting the clear meaning of the word day in Genesis 1 so man's ideas fit. This reinterpretation undermines the authority of the Bible and causes people to doubt that the Bible really is God's Word.

CONCLUSION

To finish this discussion, let's read Exodus 20:11. By the way, this passage was written by the very "finger of God":

> *For in six days the LORD made the heavens and the earth, the sea, and all that is in them, and rested the seventh day. Therefore the LORD blessed the Sabbath day and hallowed it (Exodus 20:11).*

That's where our seven-day week came from! If God worked for millions of years, and rested for millions of years, that would make nonsense of the seven-day week!

No! God created in six literal days, about 6,000 years ago, beginning with an earth of water (Genesis 1:2; 2 Peter 3:5)! How do we know it was 6,000 years ago? If you add up the genealogies from Adam to Christ, which is about 4,000 years, and add 2,000 years from the genealogies until today, it equals about 6,000 years. Billions of years and the big bang do not fit with the Bible's account of origins at all.

1 Ludwig Koehler and Walter Baumgartner, Hebrew and Aramaic Lexicon of the Old Testament, Volume 1 *(Leiden, The Netherlands: Koninklijke Brill N.V., 2001)*, p. 399.

2 Ibid.

3 James Stambaugh, "The Days of Creation: A Semantic Approach," first published in The Journal of Creation, 5, no. 1 *(April 1991)*: p. 70–78 *(later revision published by the Evangelical Theological Society)*. Online at http://www.answersingenesis.org/docs/4204tj_v5n1.asp.

Ken Ham and Bodie Hodge

Noah's ark is a fascinating ship and likely one of the most popular in all of history. **But did the ark really exist?** Could it really have housed numerous representatives of the land animal kinds for nearly a year and kept them alive during a global flood? Has it been found? These are the types of questions you are likely to hear when discussing Noah's ark with your friends.

How big was the Ark?

It was 300 cubits long, by 50 cubits wide, by 30 cubits high, according to Genesis 6:15. But how big is that? And how long is a cubit anyway? Well, there are two cubits mentioned in Scripture: an older long or royal cubit (e.g., 2 Chronicles 3:3) and a short or common cubit (e.g., Deuteronomy 3:11). Various cultures had slightly different values for their long and short cubits:

Culture	Inches (centimeters)
Hebrew *(short)*	17.5 (44.5)
Egyptian *(short)*	17.6 (44.7)
Common *(short)*	18 (45.7)
Babylonian *(long)*	19.8 (50.3)
Hebrew *(long)*	20.4 (51.8)
Egyptian *(long)*	20.6 (52.3)

Using the short 18-inch cubit, the ark would have been about **450 feet by 75 feet by 45 feet**. This is much longer than a football field. If we simply made it box shaped, here is how it would compare to a football field:

Using the royal or long cubit, the ark would be about **510 feet by 85 feet by 51 feet**.

Most ancient structures (*like the temple that Solomon built*) used the long cubit, so Noah likely used the long cubit to build the ark.

SO WAS THE ARK BOX SHAPED SINCE THE DIMENSIONS ARE SIMPLY LENGTH, WIDTH, AND HEIGHT?

The Bible doesn't say the ark was a box shape. The ark's overall dimensions are given like other ships, vehicles, and so on. For example, a Corvette ZR1's dimensions[1] are given as:

Overall Length (*in/mm*)	176.2/4476
Overall Width (*in/mm*)	75.9/1928
Overall Height (*in/mm*)	49/1244

Since these dimensions are length, width, and height, are we to assume the Corvette is a box shape? Not at all. Noah's ark was a ship and therefore, likely had features that ships would commonly have. These are not at all unreasonable assumptions. At the time Noah was constructing the ark, he was 500–600 years old and knew better than to make a simple box, because a box-shaped ship would have had significant issues in a global Flood.[2]

The ark's dimensions are unique though — falling right between strength, stability, and comfort. That is good engineering on God's part! And with fins to help guide it in the wind and waves, it would have had no major problems in a global Flood.

How many animals were on the Ark?

Most of you probably learned in biology to classify plants and animals according to the classification system of kingdom, phylum, class, order, family, genus, and species. Using this classification system, creationist researchers such as John Woodmorappe and Arthur Jones have suggested various figures for the number of animals taken on board Noah's ark:

Maximum Numbers	**Minimum** Numbers
Approximately 8,000 kinds or about 16,000 individuals *(based on the genus level of classification representing the biblical "kind")*[3] by creationist researcher John Woodmorappe	Approximately 1,000 kinds or 2,000+ individuals *(based on the family level of classification representing the biblical "kind")*[4] by Arthur J. Jones

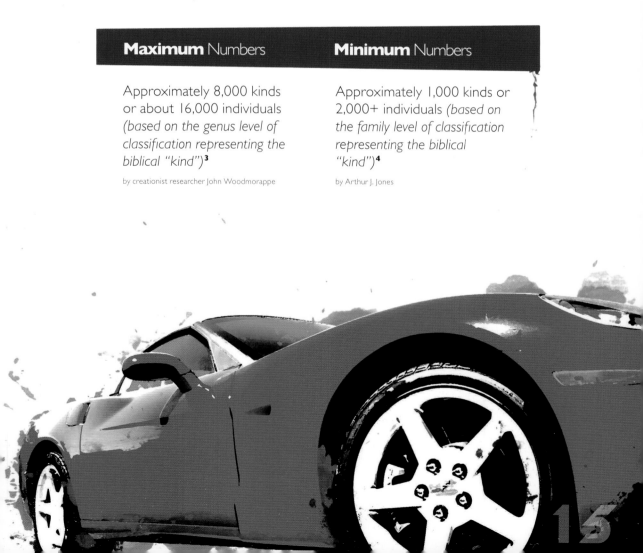

Because many creationist researchers today believe that the biblical "kind" is in most instances equated with the "family" level of classification (see more details on this further on), the number of kinds on the ark were probably closer to 1,000 to 3,000 kinds, which would be 2,000 to 6,000 individuals. Only land-dwelling, air-breathing animals were on the ark (not, for example, sea creatures) (Genesis 7:23). Research is still ongoing to try to determine the number of kinds of these land animals.

These land animal kinds were also divided into two groups: clean and unclean. The Bible states that God chose seven of each of the clean animals and two of each of the unclean to go on the ark. Even if (as some people think) there were seven pairs of each of the clean animals, rather than just seven of each of the clean animals, this really doesn't add too many extra. Incidentally, the clean animals are listed in Leviticus 11 and Deuteronomy 14. Why seven of each clean animal? Well, it seems the clean animals are those most closely associated with man (raised flocks for wool and milk, used for sacrifice, etc.), so God determined to have greater numbers of these on the ark. After the Flood, Noah sacrificed one of each of the clean animals; so more than two of each clean animal was needed for the kinds to continue to propagate. Perhaps the remaining six would have served as a good breeding stock of such animals for Noah's three sons — a pair for each of them.

WHAT IS A KIND?

The biblical word kind is considered to equate in many instances to the family level of classification. However, in some instances, it could also equate to the order, genus, or species levels, depending on the kind being considered.

To help you understand the meaning of the word kind, let's consider dogs. Even secular scientists agree that all dogs, such as dingoes, wolves, coyotes, and domestic dogs, share the same gene pool. This means there is really only one kind of dog — the dog family. Thus, only two members of the dog family were needed on Noah's ark. Similarly, it is likely that all cats (including lions, tigers, cougars, bobcats, and domestic cats) belong to one kind, and all horses (including ponies, Clydesdales, donkeys, and zebras) are their own separate kind, and so on.

Because of the great variability built into the genes of each kind, many different species have formed since the Flood as the animals spread out over the earth. **The formation of such different species is not evolution** — this just reflects the incredible variability in the genetic makeup of each kind. Biological evolution requires new information to be added into the genes, but we have never observed this! What is called "natural selection resulting in speciation" is actually just a sorting out of the genetic information already present, and it often involves the loss of information — the opposite of the supposed evolutionary process for molecules-to-man evolution.

DID ALL THE ANIMALS FIT ON THE ARK?

Let's take the worst-case scenario using John Woodmorappe's calculations with the shorter, 18-inch cubit, an ark that was 450 feet long, and the maximum number of animals (approximately 16,000, to be generous). This results in the following figures for how much of the ark space was needed:

Animal Housing	Food Inventory	Drinking Water	Open Space
46.8%	29.5%	9.4%	14.3%

Now consider the best-case scenario using a larger ark, a 20.4-inch cubit (as opposed to the 18-inch cubit), and the lesser number of animal kinds needed. These calculations show that the ark would have had plenty of room to fit the animal kinds needed. We think this second scenario was the most likely one for Noah and his family.

The dog kind: wolf   coyote   dingo   collie

Window of the Ark?

What was the window that Noah was told to build in the ark? The Hebrew word used for the window is *tsohar*, which means "noon" or "midday"; in other words, it is something that is directly overhead. It is a specialized opening at the noon or overhead position for lighting and ventilation. It runs down the top middle of something. We translate it as window, but it is more than that, like modern-day ridge vents on houses to allow ventilation and lighting.

Gopher Wood?

What kind of wood was "gopher wood"? Well, we often say, "Noah had to 'go for' a lot of wood — so it was called 'gopher' wood!" We're joking, of course. The fact is we just don't know what "gopher wood" was. Whether it was a type of wood or a means of working the wood *(e.g., styles of cross-planking — think of plywood or pressed wood)*, we are not told. For the ark, it is possible that it was a type of cross-lamination of wood like many ancient ship builders used.

In fact, the technology we see in ancient ships was likely a carryover from the Flood to Noah's descendants. After all, Noah was alive for 350 years after the Flood, and his son Shem lived 500 more years after the Flood. There were maritime/coastland peoples during the scattering at Babel (Genesis 10:5), so it would make sense that this technology was surely passed along to Noah's descendants.

Pitch?

What was the "pitch" Noah used to waterproof the ark? Pitch can be made from oil *(although the bulk of the oil we have today likely formed as a result of the Flood)* or from certain types of tree resin. The latter was likely what Noah used to obtain pitch for the ark. Pitch basically seals the ark and prevents water from coming into the ark.

Has Noah's Ark been found?

At this time, no one has found the ark yet. Some claim to have seen it and others claim to have found wood from the ark. However, nothing definitive has resulted from these supposed sightings and finds. Part of the debate is really over the question, Where did the ark land? Genesis says the ark landed on the "mountains of Ararat" — but that is a very large range of mountains (Genesis 8:4).

The current Mount Ararat is a large volcano that many creationists believe is a post-Flood volcano, because it is sitting on rock layers that were deposited by the Flood. Its last eruption was in the 1800s. The Associates for Biblical Research, an archaeology group, has an ongoing debate over where the ark landed. They published the debate in their magazine *Bible and Spade*.[5]

They argue over two places: Mt. Ararat and Mt. Cudi *(pronounced "Judi")*. Some argue for Mount Cudi because much ancient literature attests to this mountain as the ark's landing site, but others argue for modern Mount Ararat. There are pros and cons on each side. If you want to know more about the debate, the Associates for Biblical Research would be good place to start. At this point, though, nothing has been found that is definitive.

CONCLUSION

Noah's ark was real and did survive the Flood with many land animals and eight people aboard. It was able to house the animals needed to repopulate the earth, and it was well designed, so it was able survive the Flood.

So far, no one has found the ark's remains. But do not forget that our faith should not rest in finding this wooden boat *(it may not have survived after so many years of decay anyway)*. Our faith should always be in Christ and His Word, which clearly tells us that Noah's ark was real and did survive a real global Flood.

1 "Chevrolet Enters the World of Supercars with 2009 Corvette ZR1," The National Corvette Museum, http://corvettemuseum.com/specs/2009zr1/index.shtml, accessed March 23, 2012.

2 See Tim Lovett's article "Thinking Outside the Box," *Answers*, April–June 2007, for more. Also note that we are not unhappy with people who use the box-shaped ark as they are indeed closer to the biblical proportions than things like bathtub arks.

3 John Woodmorappe, *Noah's Ark: A Feasibility Study (Dallas, TX: ICR Publications, 2009)*, p. 6–10.

4 Arthur J. Jones, "How Many Animals in the Ark?" *Creation Research Society Quarterly* 10, no. 2, *(September 1973)*: p. 102–108. This was reiterated by Dr. Todd Charles Wood: ~1,000 kind or ~2,000 individuals *(based on family level)* in "Two of Every Kind," *Answers*, April–June 2007, p. 32–34.

5 *Bible and Spade*, vol. 19, no. 4, Fall 2006.

Q3 What about cavemen and

MISSING LINKS?

Dr. Tommy Mitchell

Hey, everybody knows the term "caveman," right? So what comes to mind when you hear it?

For most people, this term conjures up images of excessively hairy, stooped-over, cave-dwelling, "ape-people" wearing leopard skins and whacking their wives over the head with clubs. This is usually accompanied by the concept of these "people" grunting and discovering fire and the wheel. So it's obvious, isn't it? Surely these brutes are our ancient ancestors! Well, let's take a closer look at that story!

CAVEMEN, MISSING LINKS, AND THE TRUTH

In reality, a caveman is just someone who lives in a cave, but in this modern culture, our evolutionary indoctrination has us imagining ape-like ancestors where none exist. This is because when evolutionists refer to cavemen they are indeed talking about primitive kinds of humans who had perhaps figured out how to make simple tools or even scrawl some drawings on cave walls. They often try to figure out when these people became smart enough to make tools and draw pictures, believing their ancient ancestors were ape-like creatures that eventually evolved into humans and into all the kinds of apes we see today.

The same is true of the concept of "missing links." Missing links would theoretically be creatures sharing the ape-like ancestral characteristics with some human traits. You'll read a lot about possible missing links in the news because evolutionists believe their existence will demonstrate humans evolved from ape-like ancestors.

In reality, there are no missing links because God created human beings *(Adam and Eve)* about 6,000 years ago, just like He said He did. God did not "use evolution" to make them. Whenever skulls and skeletons of these supposed missing links are found, we know that they must be fossils either of apes or of humans, but not of any kind of transitional forms — and that is exactly what we find!

WILL THE REAL APES PLEASE STAND UP?

There have been many suggested missing links. One of the more recent ones is *Australopithecus sediba*. The discoverer of the sediba fossils even gave one of them a new name — "Karabo" — which means "the answer" to the search for humanity's most ancient missing link to our evolutionary past. Like many missing link candidates, Karabo was found in Africa.

Evolutionists believe humans first evolved in Africa, where a fair number of ape fossils have been found. This story is typical of all the missing link claims — a collection of unusual features of an ape or even of a human is interpreted to mean the owner of the bones was neither ape nor human but something in between.

Karabo is typical of other Australopithecine apes *(like the famous "Lucy")* in many ways. Evolutionists point to some features they think are unusual — like an extra long thumb or a leg bone tilted in an unusual way or an unusual indentation inside the tiny ape-shaped skull — and suggest the mixture of ape and "human" characteristics means this fossil was a transitional creature bridging the evolutionary gap to the ape-like ancestor of apes and humans. **Rather than supplying the missing link in the human evolutionary story, however, the sediba fossils look like an extinct type of tree-dwelling ape.**

But what about human fossils?

First of all, some people after the Flood didn't live in caves at all *(Noah lived in a tent)*, but burial chambers and artifacts suggesting storage or temporary shelter are often found in caves — especially as people migrate after the events at the Tower of Babel. The Cro-Magnons have typical human skeletons and have been found in caves with elaborate paintings, jewelry, and weapons. They are considered fully human.

Neanderthals also have clearly human skeletons with some variations from the typical modern human. Adult Neanderthal skulls have more prominent brow ridges and thicker bones and larger teeth than modern humans, and their overall build is stockier. **Though considered a separate species of human by secularists, DNA from Neanderthal fossils confirms they were fully human and actually intermarried with early modern humans.** Many Neanderthal tombs have been found as well as well-made stone tools and artwork in caves. Some creation scientists think Neanderthals were just one of the people groups that spread out from the Tower of Babel. Other creation scientists note that the bone thickening found in Neanderthals is typical of what would be found in people who lived for several hundred years — as people still did soon after Noah's Flood. Either way, we can be certain the Neanderthals and the Cro-Magnon were fully human descendants of Adam and Eve.

Homo erectus is another group of humans initially thought by evolutionists to be upright-walking apemen. Although the *Homo erectus* skull has a high brow ridge and a receding chin, the appearance is otherwise typical of ordinary humans. Their skeletons, tools, and evidence they hunted and used fire have been found throughout Africa, Asia, and Europe.

No DNA has been recovered from these skeletons or from the tiny *Homo floresiensis* found in Indonesia. These very short people have some unusual facial features, but also appear to be human. Recently, another yet-unnamed group of human skeletons have been found with tools and evidence they ate the extinct red deer in a cave in southwestern China. **These people also have some unusual facial and skull characteristics but are human.**

DNA has been recovered from a finger and tooth of the Denisovan people in Siberia. The two bones came from a cave in the Caucasus, and although the DNA shows they were not only human but also share genes with modern humans living in the South Pacific, no skulls or skeletons have yet been found.

Whenever evolutionists find another skull or skeleton that looks like an ape or a human, they try to add branches to the human evolutionary family tree. Although each one of these fossil finds must be either a human or an ape, sometimes there aren't enough pieces to be sure. **In fact, like a puzzle, some can look like a human or an ape depending on how you piece them together. But having a lot of missing pieces doesn't mean they should be called missing links!**

As you can see, even though humans are clearly and recognizably human, as confirmed by both DNA and the appearance of skeletons, there is a lot of variation in the way people look. But looking different does not mean they were still part ape or less evolved than other people. There are human fossils, and there are ape fossils, but there are no in-between transitional fossils.

04 But the Bible is full of
CONTRADICTIONS
...ISN'T IT?

Bodie Hodge

One of the most common attacks on the reliability of the Bible is that of alleged contradictions in Scripture! I don't know how many times I have had someone say to me, "But the Bible is full of contradictions, so how can you trust it?"

I like to ask them to "name a few" so we can discuss these allegations. I usually hear silence after that. **I've found that most people who reiterate this claim haven't really studied the subject.** If they had, they would know that these alleged contradictions in the Bible fall short over and over again.

These alleged contradictions all have reasonable explanations. Entire books have been written to refute specific alleged contradictions in the Bible, such as the *Demolishing Supposed Bible Contradictions* book series by Answers in Genesis. I'd encourage you to read that series for more in-depth explanations of supposed contradictions in Scripture. But let's take some time now to look at the basics of this topic.

Law of Non-contradiction

In the Bible, we read that God cannot lie (Titus 1:2; Hebrews 6:18; Proverbs 30:5; Psalm 18:30). This is significant because it means that God's Word will never have contradictions. Though skeptics have alleged that there are contradictions in the Bible, such claims are easily refuted when they are studied. This is what we would expect when we consider that God's Word is perfect.

A legitimate contradiction is labeled with this fancy statement: "A cannot equal not-A at the same time and in the same relationship." This is called the "law of non-contradiction." Let me give you an example: I cannot be sitting at my computer at 9:46 a.m. at 15 seconds after the minute, February 16, 2012, and NOT be sitting at my computer at 9:46 AM at 15 seconds after the minute, February 16, 2012! That would be a sight to see, wouldn't it?

But could I be sitting at my computer and not sitting at my computer at two different times? Yes, of course. Even though it is the same thing and in the same relationship, it is happening at two different times, so it is not a contradiction. Could I be sitting at my computer and at the same time be looking at my door? Yes. Could I be in my office and be sitting at my computer at the same time? Yes. Could I be sitting at my computer and at the same time someone else be sitting at my computer? Yes. We both could be sitting there and this is not a contradiction. For a legitimate contradiction, I must be there and not be there at the same time in the same situation.

Now that you know what a contradiction really is, let's see the types of alleged contradictions that people claim about the Bible.

COMMON TYPES OF ALLEGED CONTRADICTIONS

These are some of the common categories of alleged contradictions:

- **Inferring a contradiction** (*bad assumptions*): When people claim there is a contradiction that is not stated in the text, they infer a contradiction. For example, someone might infer a contradiction by saying that the Israelites couldn't both be in Egypt (Genesis 47:27) and be in the Promised Land (Joshua 22:4). Of course the Israelites were in both places, but at different times.

- **Factual contradiction** (*got their facts wrong*): When someone says the Bible is false because of "facts" about the world that turn out to be false, this is a factual contradiction. Consider if someone says the Bible is in contradiction (Genesis 1) with the well-known "fact of evolution",..they obviously don't realize that evolution is not a fact, but a false worldview. Or think of it this way: suppose someone claims the Bible has a contradiction when it says that God is the only one who is omnipresent (*i.e., everywhere at once, not bound by time*) because Santa Claus also must be omnipresent to deliver all those presents at the same time on Christmas Eve! Santa's existence is not a fact at all; therefore, there is no contradiction with Scripture.

- **Issues in translation**: Sometimes words can be translated better. But many times alleged contradictions can be avoided through careful word studies and making sure we honor the author's meaning. For example, some people criticize Moses for calling a bat a "bird" (Leviticus 11:13–19), but really he didn't. The Hebrew word we translate as bird literally means "winged creature." So even though the translators chose to use "bird" in Leviticus 11, Moses' original meaning was "winged creatures," which includes bats and birds.

- **Generalizations**: Some people try to say that a generalization about something must be true in every situation, no matter what. Think of it like this: if your mom says, "Stay away from the cookies," does that mean that you must stay away from all the cookies at all times all around the world? No! Your mom definitely wants you to stay away from the cookies she just baked, but she did not indicate that you couldn't eat cookies at a friend's house. In the Bible, God commands us not to kill (more specifically, murder) people. So is it wrong to kill in every circumstance, no matter what? No! There are exceptions in Scripture where killing in self-defense, killing as punishment for a crime, and killing in war are permitted. Many alleged contradictions result when people make a generalization in Scripture the rule in every situation without exception. Exceptions to a general rule are not contradictions.

- **Contextual contradiction** *(out of context)*: Using Bible verses out of context is one the most common ways people use to create contradictions. I once had someone claim that one passage of the Bible says "there is a God," but that Psalm 14:1 says "there is no God." But when you look up Psalm 14:1, it actually says, "The fool has said in his heart, 'There is no God.' " In context, Psalm 14:1 isn't saying God doesn't exist, but that only a "fool" says there is no God. Clearly, this is not a contradiction.

- **False dilemma**: When someone sets up situation where two things that normally work together are treated as thought they can't, you have a false dilemma. For example, someone might say that the Bible was either inspired by God or written by man. But the fact is it was both! God used human authors, but He inspired them to write what He wanted written.

- **Copyist errors**: When the Bible was originally written by its inspired authors *(Moses, David, Peter, Paul, and others)*, it was inerrant *(without flaws or mistakes)*. But since then, people have made copies of it, and sometimes we see copyist mistakes. The few mistakes we see make little if any difference to theology. In some cases, these changes were likely deliberate, like updating a word that was out of date or not used any longer. The good thing is that we have so many ancient copies of the Scriptures *(for example, we have over 5,300 copies or Greek sections of the New Testament)*. This means that by comparing these copies, it is easy to see when someone made a copy mistake. But this has caused a handful of alleged contradictions. A common one is that the name Cainan was copied an extra time in the Genesis genealogies that Luke reiterated in Luke 3:36. It looks like a contradiction when compared with Genesis 5 or 1 Chronicles 1. Some early copies of Luke do not have this extra Cainan, however, so many scholars see this as an obvious copyist mistake.

There are other types of alleged contradictions, but this list covers many of them.

Can non-Christians appeal to contradictions?

If there is no God and everything is material, then we have a big problem! Logic is not made up of material *(the law of non-contradiction is abstract and has no mass for example)*, so if everything is material, then "so what" if someone contradicts himself? Furthermore, who would care in 900 trillion years anyway in their worldview?

But here's the interesting part: the sheer fact that atheists (and humanists, skeptics, and others) try to appeal to laws of logic actually undermines their own position! Where does logic come from? It comes from God's self-consistent nature. God doesn't contradict Himself, and He upholds the universe. When non-Christians appeal to logic as a way of arguing against the Bible, they are really appealing to the truthfulness of the Bible, which teaches that contradictions are wrong. So when non-Christians appeal to alleged contradictions in the Bible, they are really saying their own worldview is wrong and the Bible's is right...they just don't realize it. Since the Bible is where we find the basis for the law of non-contradiction, then it is through a biblical worldview that we can know that these contradictions are false.

Don't fossils prove

EVOLUTION?

Dr. Tommy Mitchell

You've probably heard that the evolutionary progress of one kind of animal evolving into another can be seen in the fossil record. You may have even heard that the transitional forms that allegedly prove this sort of evolution happened are right there in the rocks for all to see.

And you've most likely seen pictures of the geologic column — layers of rocks full of fossils supposedly providing a visual time-line of millions of years of evolutionary progress. Let's consider what the fossil record really does and does not contain and see what that alleged time-line "written" in the rocks is really telling us.

ISN'T THE ORDER OF THE FOSSILS IN THE ROCK LAYERS PROOF OF EVOLUTION?

All over the world we find sedimentary rock layers containing fossils — the remains of organisms of all sizes that have been buried, mineralized, and preserved. Supposedly laid down over millions of years, those layers, according to evolutionists and long agers, preserve for us the record of what sorts of plants and animals had evolved at different times in earth's history.

Essentially, the deepest layers of all — the Precambrian — contain no fossils other than those of some microbes. Then above that is Cambrian rock. Since the layer below the Cambrian lacks fossils while the Cambrian is packed with them, evolutionists say the "Cambrian explosion" happened — the sudden evolution of lots of creatures.

As a general order, Cambrian rock is supposedly 540 million years old and contains an enormous variety of fossils, mostly marine invertebrates — the kind of creatures typically found near the ocean bottom. Farther up in the Devonian layers we begin to see fish fossils. Then come amphibians, then some reptiles, then mammals and dinosaurs and flowers, and finally birds. Human fossils are hard to find but they tend to be scattered only in uppermost layers. Land vertebrates make their appearance much higher in the rock layers than marine organisms.

Although evolutionists insist these living things evolved in the order they were buried, no undisputed transitional forms *(intermediate kinds of organisms showing how one kind evolved into another)* are found. **None.**

Yet evolutionists tell us transitional forms were involved in the evolution of each and every kind of living thing on the earth. Shouldn't the fossil record contain a lot of them? *(In fact, there should be a whole lot of them. If evolution were true, there should be many, many more fossils of these in-between creatures than fossils of fully formed creatures.)*

Some evolutionists explain this absence by saying evolution happened too rapidly to preserve the transitions, but they also say we can't see evolution happening right now because it happens too slowly. So what is it — fast or slow? It can't be too fast to see and too slow to see, can it?

LAYERS ARE THE ORDER OF BURIAL DURING THE FLOOD!

There is a real order in the fossil record, but what is that order telling us? To get a clue, let's consider how those fossils and layers of rock formed. Not every death or burial produces a fossil. To be fossilized, an organism needs to be rapidly buried to shut off the oxygen supply to bacteria in its tissues and thus prevent rotting. It also needs some significant mineral content in the water so that the dead thing can be mineralized and turned into what amounts to long-lasting rock.

Evolutionists tell us the layers of sediment that eventually hardened into rock were laid down over millions of years. If that were true, then how did all those dead things get buried fast enough not to rot and decay?

Can you think of an event in history that could have caused rapid burial of billions of organisms all over the world? How about a global Flood?
The Bible describes the Flood of Noah's day as a cataclysmic upheaval with much associated volcanic activity that broke open "the fountains of the deep," about 4,300 years ago.

We can imagine that over the weeks in which the floodwaters rose there were violent waves due to this volcanic activity. Those upheavals would have first affected the organisms living deep in the oceans, stirring up the sediment on the ocean bottom and burying billions of marine creatures in the Cambrian rock layers — right from the start!

As the waters rose higher, they sequentially wrecked the habitats of creatures and buried many. **The order we see in the fossil record is a record of the order in which organisms were buried.** We see fish first, then creatures and plants that would have been found in more low-lying areas of the pre-Flood world, then finally creatures able to temporarily flee from the surges of ocean waves sweeping over the land.

We even find the fossilized tracks of some of these creatures preserved by the mineral-rich sediment, which acted like quick-set concrete to preserve them. Finally catching up to the inland areas, the rising water overwhelmed those animals initially able to flee *(larger dinosaurs, mammals, and birds)* as well as the plants indigenous to higher elevations, such as flowers.

The very top layers of sedimentary rock include fossils of some creatures and people buried in catastrophic local flooding events in the hundreds of years after the Flood when the world had begun to be repopulated. **Most of the fossil record is actually a time-line of the awful year of the global Flood. But none of the fossil record is a record of the evolution of life.**

Q6 Isn't Natural Selection Evolution?

MY TEXTBOOK SAYS THEY'RE THE SAME

Dr. Tommy Mitchell

Natural selection and evolution are not the same thing, but evolutionists, beginning with Charles Darwin, say that natural selection is the "driving force" behind evolution. To make things more complicated, evolution is a slippery word with several different scientific definitions. **Once we define these terms, the truth should be clear.**

Ready? Let's get to it!

WHAT IS NATURAL SELECTION?

Natural selection is sometimes called "survival of the fittest." When a group of living things is faced with an environmental challenge (*like drought or cold or changes in the food supply*), the individuals best equipped to survive in that environment are most likely to survive and to have a chance to reproduce. Simple examples would be, say, creatures with long fur surviving better in cold environments or animals with good camouflage surviving better than those with none.

When the survivors reproduce, their offspring will inherit various characteristics from the parents, including those traits that equipped the parents to survive. Over time, the less fit members of the population — whether plants or animals or bacteria — will be unable to pass on their genes before they die. Thus, the population will become much like the fittest parents. We say that nature selected the fitter members of the population to survive and reproduce themselves. We say that in spite of the fact that nature cannot select anything. See why the terms are confusing?

The new population — after natural selection happens — contains less genetic diversity than the original population (*because the less useful characteristics eventually are lost from the gene pool*), but it is better suited to the environment. Of course, if the environment changes drastically again, the new population may not have the genetic traits that would allow it to adapt to the new conditions because the population has less information in its genes. Also, the new population is only a variation of the original one, not a whole new kind of organism.

But didn't Charles Darwin discover natural selection?

Many people think Charles Darwin discovered natural selection. But actually a creationist named Edward Blyth figured out how natural selection works 22 years before Darwin published his famous book about evolution. Blyth published his ideas in the *Magazine of Natural History* between 1835 and 1837. Darwin even had copies of the magazines.

Blyth understood that God had created the original kinds of plants and animals. Adam's sin brought the curse of death into God's perfect creation. Blyth understood natural selection was a way diverse populations could develop to suit different sorts of environments in the sin-cursed world.

Also, natural selection would result in many instances in the weaker animals and plants dying off, leaving the stronger ones to reproduce. This became especially important after the global Flood, when many variations of the originally created kinds were needed to fill each ecological niche in the changing world.

Darwin did not believe what God said about the way He had made the world. God's eyewitness record in Genesis says He created all kinds of animals and plants to reproduce after their kind. *(That means dogs produce dogs and bacteria produce bacteria and dinosaurs produced dinosaurs, but dinosaurs did not produce birds.)*

But Darwin thought of a way to ignore God. Darwin decided life started all by itself from the chemicals that made up the earth. He believed that simple life forms developed and gradually got more and more complex, forming ancestors for all sorts of plants and animals and microbes and humans. We call this "molecules-to-man" evolution, or "goo-to-you" evolution. There is no way for living things to randomly form themselves from non-living things. This has never ever been observed or discovered and is even a law of biology — the law of biogenesis. Living things only come from living things.

Darwin thought that natural selection — the gradual selection of the fittest life forms for survival — resulted in the formation of more complex organisms. However, the result of natural selection is only the re-sorting of the genetic information (the genes) already in an organism. Natural selection does not result in new information or provide living things with the blueprints to become something more complicated.

Ultimately with natural selection, genetic information is lost in a population so that the organisms are variations of their parents, but not new and more complex kinds; but after new combinations of existing information. **Thus, the process of natural selection cannot drive molecules-to-man evolution or even the evolution of more complex kinds of organisms from simpler ancestors.**

ISN'T NATURAL SELECTION JUST A FORM OF EVOLUTION?

Remember, we said evolution is a slippery word with more than one definition. The word evolution can simply mean "change." So while simple organisms do not evolve into more complex ones, the characteristics of a kind of living thing can vary. *(For example, there are many varieties of dogs, but they're all dogs.)* Through the process of natural selection, this happens.

After the world was devastated by the global Flood and the environment began to stabilize, there were many habitats to be filled. The animals that survived the Flood on Noah's ark multiplied and spread over the world. As they moved into different habitats, those best suited for each ecological niche survived to reproduce and repopulate the world. But because there were many different kinds of habitats, natural selection of the fittest resulted in many different varieties of living things — but this is not evolution in the grander sense of the word.

Because we do see what is called "natural selection" in nature — sometimes even producing new species of some plants and animals in just a few years — some people say we can see "evolution in action." And since they see that kind of change — or "evolution" — happening, they believe millions of years of natural selection could cause more complex living things to evolve from simple ones.

However, natural selection does not result in more complex information. **Natural selection can only select from the genetic information already existing in each kind of organism.** Therefore, we observe natural selection in the real world, but to say we see "evolution in action" is a careless and ambiguous use of words that leads to wrong conclusions.

Q7 Mutations are good for evolution, right? I mean,

X-MEN CAN'T BE WRONG,

can it?

Dr. Tommy Mitchell

"Professor Xavier" wrong? Say it ain't so!

WHAT ARE MUTATIONS?

Mutations are changes in genes. Mutations — the spontaneous changes that occur by accident in the genes of living things — sometimes cause altered characteristics that can make the organism more or less fit to survive. Evolutionists believe that if enough mutations happen for long enough, new and more complicated organisms evolve.

Mutations are like mistakes. So evolutionists believe enough mistakes for long enough can add up to the information to make new kinds of organisms. The *X-Men* movies *(as well as many entertaining shows like Spiderman, Heroes, Ninja Turtles, and so on)* are based on the idea that mutations produced individuals with superpowers.

The chromosomes inside cells contain many genes. Those genes make up the blueprint, or instructions, for all the physical characteristics of that organism, whether it is a bacterium or a tree or a cat.

When a bacterium reproduces, it simply divides and makes copies of itself, mutations and all. But when a more complex animal reproduces, it only passes on the information in its "germ cells." Eggs and sperm are germ cells. Only mutations in the genes of the germ cells get passed on to offspring.

If those same mutations exist in all the cells of an organism, then the characteristics produced by those traits may have helped the organism survive in a particular environment to reproduce.

43

Mutations and Sickle Cell Anemia!

But wait a minute — didn't we say mutations are mistakes? Yes, they are. *(Again with apologies to Professor Xavier.)* And when a mutation happens, a normal gene becomes abnormal and information is lost. However, in certain environments, a particular mutation might be a good thing for survival. A good example is "sickle cell trait."

Sickle cell anemia is an inherited disease of the blood caused by a mutation. Many people die from sickle cell anemia. However, if a person only inherits the sickle mutation from one parent, half of the person's blood hemoglobin will be normal. Therefore, half of his red blood cells will work properly.

People with this "sickle cell trait" are more likely to survive malaria infections *(a major health problem in parts of Africa)* than normal people. Malaria is a parasite that hijacks human red blood cells to reproduce itself. Malaria doesn't reproduce itself as well in people with sickle cell trait. Thus, people with that mutation actually survive better in malaria-infested places than unaffected people.

But do you see that the people with sickle trait are not evolving to become a new kind of human? And people with sickle cell trait can have children with sickle cell anemia, a very bad disease. Thus, survival is improved for people with sickle trait in malaria-infested places, but the population as a whole suffers instead of "evolving" into a healthier population. And no one in the population is evolving into a more advanced kind of human.

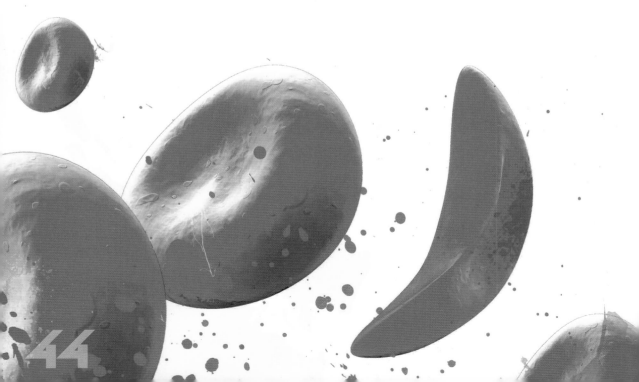

Antibiotic Resistance - Isn't That a Good One?

What about antibiotic resistance? You've probably heard that antibiotic resistance is "evolution in action." But remember, molecules-to-man evolution and the evolution of more complex organisms from simpler ancestors would require the addition of new genetic information... but this is what we never observe happening. Let's see what happens to produce antibiotic-resistant bacteria. You'll see that nothing new evolves and no new information is created.

Although most bacteria in the world, and even in your body, are helpful, some cause disease. Antibiotics can be used to treat many of these diseases, killing large numbers of the disease-causing bacteria. But if the bacteria causing a disease are resistant to a particular antibiotic, the antibiotic won't help. In hospitals where lots of antibiotics are used, it seems like "superbugs" evolve — populations of bacteria resistant to all the common antibiotics. **But did the bacteria really evolve?**

Antibiotics usually attack bacteria by interfering with some necessary process in the bacteria's life. Some bacteria harbor genes that give them a "work-around" for the targeted process. Those bacteria are already resistant to certain antibiotics. Therefore, when antibiotics kill off their neighbors, the survivors multiply to produce a resistant population.

But where did those bacteria with the "resistance genes" get their information? Sometimes bacteria are resistant because they already have a mutation — an abnormality — in the gene coding for the protein normally attacked by an antibiotic. Since that bacterium produces only a variation of the target protein, the antibiotic is unable to attack it. Sometimes, they are resistant because they already had the information to begin with.

Bacteria also are able to acquire genetic information for various traits by passing genetic information between themselves. **This only happens between micro-organisms like bacteria, not in multi-cellular organisms.** And the genetic information being passed around is still bacterial information, not the information to evolve into a multi-cellular organism like a lizard or a mouse. Thus, no new information is being created, only shuffled around between bacteria.

And the bacteria that happened to have been dealt some resistance genes are able to survive when attacked with modern medicine's antibiotic arsenal. Then they reproduce to build a resistant population.

Proof that antibiotic resistance represents only the natural selection of information already present in bacteria and not evolution to escape antibiotic attack was found in Arctic ice. Explorers who died and were buried there many years before any antibiotics were invented were later found to have bacteria resistant to modern antibiotics in their bodies. Those bacteria had the genes to resist the antibiotics even though they had never before been exposed to them.

So, the bacteria in the new population are the same kind of bacteria with minor — though extremely useful — variations. But since they now survive antibiotic attacks, shouldn't we give them credit for evolving a stronger population? No. Those bacteria may be better equipped to survive in the presence of antibiotics, but alterations in the target proteins represent a loss of information, and in a different environment that mutation offers no survival advantage at all. **In fact, they are generally weaker than the original variety.**

Conclusion

No new information is created by mutations. New mutant populations result from a reshuffling of pre-existing information. That's not evolution; it's just natural selection. This is the mechanism God put in place to produce genetic variability within the created kinds.

So while the *X-Men* movies are fun to watch, we should remember that real mutations do not produce new and better individuals. Mutations cannot provide the raw material for evolution to a more advanced kind of human or a more advanced kind of anything else.

WHAT MAKES IT SO SPECIAL?

Bodie Hodge

All Scripture is given by inspiration of God, and is profitable for doctrine, for reproof, for correction, for instruction in righteousness, that the man of God may be complete, thoroughly equipped for every good work (2 Timothy 3:16–17).

It truly is a secular age. I had the opportunity to be at a state school a couple of years ago to give a lecture for a student-led club. I began answering some questions that the students had at the end of the lecture. Even though there was a very negative tone coming from many of the questioners, I remained courteous in each response.

Most of the questions were common and fairly easy to answer. The questions began with the creation-evolution debate, dealing with dinosaurs and radiometric dating. After those were answered, the questions became more impassioned and were directed toward God and the Bible: "Who created God?" and "Isn't the Bible full of contradictions?" At the end, one question came up that I did not have an opportunity to answer. A student asked, "Was the Bible written by men?" The bell rang and out they went. **I wished this question had come up sooner, because it gets much closer to the heart of the biblical authority issue.**

So What Is the Answer?

When it comes to the authorship of the Bible, of course humans were involved. Christians would be the first to point this out. For example, Paul wrote letters to early churches that are included in the Scriptures (2 Peter 3:15–16). David wrote many of the Psalms. Moses wrote the Pentateuch, or the Torah (*the first five books of the Bible*). In fact, it is estimated that over 40 different human authors were involved. So human authorship is not the issue.

The issue is this: did God have any involvement or not? Second Peter 1:21 says, "for prophecy never came by the will of man, but holy men of God spoke as they were moved by the Holy Spirit." Did God move the authors of the inspired Scriptures? Yes (2 Timothy 3:16). When someone claims that the Bible was written by men and not God, this is an absolute statement that reveals something extraordinary.

It reveals that the person saying this is claiming to be transcendent! When someone claims that God was not moving the human authors of the Bible, that person is claiming to be omniscient, omnipresent, and omnipotent!

1. **Omniscient:** they are claiming to be an all-knowing authority on the subject of God's inspiration, to refute God's claim that Scripture was inspired by Him (2 Timothy 3:16).

2. **Omnipresent:** they are claiming that they were present, both spiritually and physically, to observe that God had no part in aiding any of the biblical authors.

3. **Omnipotent:** they are claiming that if God had tried to help the biblical authors, then they had the power to stop such an action.

So the person making the claim that the Bible was written by men is claiming to be God; but these three attributes belong solely to God. This is a religious issue of humanism versus Christianity. The person is claiming (*perhaps inadvertently*) that he is the ultimate authority over God and is trying to convince you that God is subservient to him. This needs to be addressed when responding to him.

WHAT IS A GOOD RESPONSE?

I like to respond in ways that reveal this issue in a question — and there are several ways to do it. For example, you can address omnipresence by asking, "Do you really believe that you are omnipresent? The only way for you to prove that God had no involvement in the writing of the Scriptures is for you to be omnipresent." Then point out that he was claiming to be God, even if he didn't realize it, when he made the statement that God had no involvement in the Bible.

You can always lead them down the path by first asking an easier question: **"How do you know that God was not involved?"** But then you will have to listen to their response in order to know how to proceed after that.

Another method of responding is to undercut the entire position by pointing out that any type of reasoning apart from the Bible is merely arbitrary. The person trying to make a logical argument against the claims of the Bible (*i.e., that God inspired the authors*) does so assuming that logic and truth exist — but logic and truth exist only if the Bible is true! In order for his presupposition (*i.e., logic and truth exist*) to be reliable, the Bible has to be true. It is helpful to point out these types of presuppositions and inconsistencies.

Someone may respond: "What if I claim that Shakespeare was inspired by God — then you would have to be omniscient, omnipresent, and omnipotent to refute it."

Actually, it is irrelevant for me to be omniscient, omnipresent, and omnipotent to refute it. God, who is omniscient, omnipresent, and omnipotent, refutes this claim from what He has already stated in the Bible. Nowhere did God self-authenticate Shakespeare's writings as Scripture. However, Christ, the Creator-God (John 1; Colossians 1; Hebrews 1), approved the Old Testament prophetic works and the New Testament apostolic works. The 66 books of the Bible were already sealed (*see the chapter on the 66 books of the Bible in this book*).

CONCLUSION

Sadly, in today's society, children *(churched or not)* are being heavily exposed to the religion of humanism, which reigns in state schools. So it is logical that the next generation would be thinking in terms of humanism and apply that to the Bible.

The student about whom I previously spoke was applying the religion of humanism *(i.e., man is the authority, not God)* to the Bible when he claimed that it was written merely by men. He viewed himself as the authority and not God. He further reasoned that there is no God at all, and therefore, the Bible could not have had God's involvement. Therefore, his statement that the Bible was written by men was a religious claim — he was claiming to be God. Many follow this same thought process but fail to realize its implications and problems.

If one can expose the false religion of humanism, then others may be more open to realizing the deception. After all, the person is not the enemy; rather, it is the false principalities and dark powers that are at work trying to deceive (Ephesians 6:12) that we must demolish (2 Corinthians 10:5).

Q9 How should I interpret

THE BIBLE?

Ken Ham & Bodie Hodge

Sometimes people ask why creationists take the Bible "literally." Saying creationists take the Bible "literally" is not a bad thing, but it may be better to say that creationists read and understand the Bible according to the "grammatical-historical" approach to Scripture which means to take it "naturally."

Don't let the big term scare you! The "grammatical-historical" approach means, simply put, that we understand a biblical passage by taking into account its context, author, readership, and literary style. In other words, we read and understand the Bible in a plain or straightforward manner. This is usually what people mean when they say "literal interpretation of the Bible." This method helps to eliminate improper interpretations of the Bible. Consider what the Bible says here:[1]

But we have renounced disgraceful, underhanded ways. We refuse to practice cunning or to tamper with God's word, but by the open statement of the truth we would commend ourselves to everyone's conscience in the sight of God (2 Corinthians 4:2).

All the words of my mouth are righteous; there is nothing twisted or crooked in them. They are all straight to him who understands, and right to those who find knowledge (Proverbs 8:8–9).

These two passages tell us that Scripture is truthful, so we should seek to understand passages in the Bible by carefully studying them, not by forcing our own meanings on them. Reading the Bible "plainly" means understanding which passages are written as historical narrative, which are written as poetry, which are written as parable, which are written as prophecy, and so on. The Bible is written in many different literary styles and should be read accordingly. **Genesis records actual historical events;** it was written as historical narrative, and there is no reason to read it as any other literary style, such as allegory or poetry.

Context, Context!

For example, a non-Christian once claimed, "The Bible clearly says 'there is no God' in Psalm 14:1." However, this verse in context says:

The fool says in his heart, "There is no God." They are corrupt, they do abominable deeds, there is none who does good (Psalm 14:1).

The context helps determine the proper interpretation — that a fool claims there is no God.

Someone else claimed, "To interpret the days in Genesis, you need to read 2 Peter 3:8, which indicates the days are each a thousand years." Many people try to use this passage to support the idea that the earth is millions or billions of years old, but let's read it in context:

But do not overlook this one fact, beloved, that with the Lord one day is as a thousand years, and a thousand years as one day. The Lord is not slow to fulfill his promise as some count slowness, but is patient toward you, not wishing that any should perish, but that all should reach repentance (2 Peter 3:8–9).

This passage employs a literary device called a simile. Here, God compares a day to a thousand years in order to make the point that time doesn't bind Him, in this case specifically regarding His patience. A strict "literal" reading would require us to say that God's days are a thousand years — but that is theologically inaccurate since God is not bound by time! When we consider the literary style and the context, this passage tells us that God is eternal and is not limited to the time He created.

These verses also do not reference the days in Genesis, so we cannot reasonably apply this to the length of the days in Genesis 1. **When read plainly, these verses indicate that God is patient when keeping His promises.** The gentleman who spoke about this passage had preconceived beliefs based on man's ideas that the earth was millions of years old. Because this gentleman believed man's ideas about the age of the earth, he doubted the words of Scripture. His doubt led him try to make Genesis 1 fit with the ideas he already had as opposed to using the historical-grammatical method to see what Genesis 1 plainly says about the creation days.

Conclusion

Creationists who follow the historical-grammatical method read the Bible plainly, or straightforwardly, and in context. They consider the context, author, readership, and literary style of each biblical passage, and they do not try to force passages to fit with their own preconceived notions. By following this method, we learn from what God says and means, and we don't apply strange literalistic (in the strict sense) meanings to metaphorical or allegorical passages, nor do we apply allegorical or metaphorical meanings to passages that should be read literally. **Reading the Bible using the historical-grammatical approach means that we believe the words of Scripture, rather than doubting them, and this belief is the basis of our Christian faith.**

1 All passages in this chapter are from the ESV.

Q10 But doesn't the Bible support

SLAVERY?

Bodie Hodge[1]

The issue of slavery usually conjures up thoughts of the harsh "race"-based slavery[2] that was common by Europeans toward those of African descent in the latter few centuries. However, slavery has a much longer history and needs to be addressed biblically. **If you have a Bible, you may want to use it as you read this chapter.** You'll be able to understand what the Bible says about slavery better if you look up and read the passages as I discuss them. So what does the Bible really teach about slavery?

BRIEF HISTORY OF SLAVERY

It is important to note that neither slavery in New Testament times nor slavery under the Mosaic covenant have anything to do with the sort of slavery where African peoples were bought and sold as property by European and American peoples in the well-known slave trade of the last few centuries. The type of slavery the Mosaic covenant refers to and that was practiced in New Testament times was starkly different and few realize that unless they study the subject. Harsh slavery is not a recent invention, however, and the United States and the United Kingdom were not the only countries in history to delve into harsh slavery and so be stained.

1. The Code of Hammurabi discussed slavery soon after 2242 B.C. *(the date assigned by Archbishop Ussher to the Tower of Babel incident).*

2. Ham's son Mizraim founded Egypt *(still called Mizraim in Hebrew).* Egypt was the first well-documented nation in the Bible to have harsh slavery, which was imposed on Joseph, the son of Israel, in 1728 B.C. *(according to Archbishop Ussher).* Later, the Egyptians were slave masters to the rest of the Israelites, but Moses, by the hand of God, freed them.

3. The Israelites were again enslaved by Assyrian and Babylonian captors about 1,000 years later.

4. African Moors enslaved Europeans during their conquering of Spain and Portugal on the Iberian Peninsula in the 8th century A.D. for over 400 years. The Moors even took slaves as far north as Scandinavia. The Moorish and Middle Eastern slave market was quite extensive.

5. Norse raiders of Scandinavia *(e.g., Sweden and Norway)* enslaved other European peoples and took them back as property beginning in the 8th century A.D.

6. Even in modern times, slavery is still alive in Africa such as in the Sudan and Darfur as well as human trafficking in many parts of the world, too.

We find many other examples of harsh slavery from cultures throughout the world. At any rate, these few examples indicate that harsh slavery was/is a reality, and in all cases, is an unacceptable act by biblical standards *(as we will see)*.

WHAT ABOUT SLAVERY IN THE BIBLE?

Was slavery in the Bible the same as harsh slavery? For example, slaves and masters are referred to in Paul's epistles. In Ephesians 6:5, a better translation of the word slave is the word "bondservant."

The Bible is in no way giving full support to the practice of bondservants, who were certainly not being paid the first century equivalent of the minimum wage. Nevertheless, they were being paid something (Colossians 4:1) and were therefore in something more like a lifetime employment contract rather than "racial" slavery. Moreover, Paul gives clear instructions that Christian "masters" are to treat such people with respect and as equals. Their employment position did not affect their standing in the Church.

As we already know, harsh slavery was common in the Middle East and Africa as far back as ancient Egypt. If God had simply ignored it, then there would have been no rules for the treatment of slaves/bondservants, and they could have treated them harshly with no rights. But the God-given rights and rules for their protection showed that God cared for them as well.

This is often mistaken as an endorsement of harsh slavery, which it is not. God listed slave traders among the worst of sinners in 1 Timothy 1:10 *(kidnappers/men stealers/slave traders)*. This is not a new teaching, as Moses was not fond of forced slavery either:

He who kidnaps a man and sells him, or if he is found in his hand, shall surely be put to death (Exodus 21:16).

In fact, take note of the punishment of Egypt, when the Lord freed the Israelites (Exodus chapters 3–15). God predicted this punishment well in advance in Genesis 15:13–14.

Had God not protected slaves/bondservants by such commands, then many people surrounding them who did have harsh slavery would have loved to move in where there were no governing principles as to the treatment of slaves. It would have given a "green light" to slave owners from neighboring areas to come and settle there. But with the rules in place, it discouraged such slavery in their realm.

In fact, the laws and regulations over slavery are a sure sign that slavery isn't good in the same way the Law came to expose and limit sin (Romans 5:13). One reverend said it this way:

In giving laws to regulate slavery, God is not saying it is a good thing. In fact, by giving laws about it at all, He is plainly stating it is a bad thing. We don't make laws to limit or regulate good things. After all, you won't find laws that tell us it is wrong to be too healthy or that if water is too clean we have to add pollution to it. Therefore, the fact slavery is included in the regulations of the Old Testament at all assumes that it is a bad thing which needs regulation to prevent the damage from being too great.[3]

Aren't There Verses That Support Harsh Slavery?

There are several passages that are commonly used to suggest that the Bible supports harsh slavery. However, when we read these passages in context, we find that they clearly oppose harsh slavery. You'll understand the context of these passages if you read them for yourself as we discuss them.

Consider Exodus 21:2–6. This is the first type of "bankruptcy law" we've encountered. With this, a government doesn't step in, but a person who has lost himself to debt can sell the only thing he has left: his ability to perform labor. This is a loan. In six years the loan is paid off, and he is set free. Bondservants who did this made a wage, had their debt covered, had a home to stay in, on-the-job training, and did it for only six years. This almost sounds better than college, which doesn't cover debt and you have to pay for it!

This is not a forced agreement either. The bondservants enter into service voluntarily. In the same respect, a foreigner can sell himself into servitude, too. Although the rules are slightly different, it would still be by the foreigner's own choice in light of Exodus 21:16 (*servants who were conquered in war also had some slightly different rules*).

Consider Exodus 21:18–21. This passage follows closely after Moses' decree against slave traders in Exodus 21:16. The rules still apply for their protection if they already have servants or if someone sells himself/herself into service.

Consider Leviticus 25:38–46. God prefaces this passage specifically with a reminder that the Lord saved them from their bondage of slavery in Egypt. Again, if a person becomes poor, he or she can sell himself/herself into slavery/servitude and be released as was already discussed.

Sadly, some Israelite kings later tried to institute forced slavery, for example Solomon (1 Kings 9:15) and Rehoboam with Adoniram (1 Kings 12:18). Both fell from favor in God's sight and were found to follow after evil (1 Kings 11:6; 2 Chronicles 12:14).

Consider Luke 12:43–48. As for Christ's supposed support for beating slaves, this is in the context of a parable. Parables are stories Jesus told to help us understand spiritual truths. For example, in one parable, Jesus likens God to a judge (Luke 18:1–5). The judge is unjust, but eventually gives justice to the widow when she persists. The point of that story was not to tell us that God is like an unjust judge — on the contrary, He is completely just. The point of the parable is to tell us to be persistent in prayer. Similarly, Luke 12:47–48 does not justify beating slaves. It is not a parable telling us how masters are to behave. It is a parable telling us that we must be ready for when Jesus Himself returns. One will be rewarded with eternal life through Christ, or with eternal punishment (Matthew 25:46).

Consider Ephesians 6:5–9. Again, Paul in Ephesians is not giving an endorsement to slavery/bondservants and masters, but he gives them both the same commands, showing that God views them as equals in Christ. Furthermore, Paul says in Colossians 4:1 that bondservants were to be paid fair wages.

CONCLUSION

Though this short chapter couldn't delve into every verse regarding slavery, the basic principles are the same. In light of what we've learned, here are a few pointers to remember:

1. Slaves under Mosaic Law were different from the harshly treated slaves of other societies; they were more like servants or bondservants. Today, people still hire maids and butlers and this is fairly similar.

2. The Bible doesn't give an endorsement of slave traders but the opposite (1 Timothy 1:10). A slave/bondservant was acquired when a person voluntarily entered into it when he needed to pay off his debts.

3. The Bible recognizes that slavery is a reality in this sin-cursed world and doesn't ignore it, but instead gives regulations for good treatment by both masters and servants and reveals that they are equal under Christ.

4. Israelites could sell themselves as slaves/bondservants to have their debts covered, make a wage, have housing, and be set free after six years. Foreigners could sell themselves as slaves/bondservants as well.

5. Many forget that it was biblical Christians like William Wilberforce and Abraham Lincoln who led the fight to abolish harsh slavery in modern times.

Now that you understand what slavery looked like in the Bible, consider this regarding Christ. When you have a debt so big that you could never pay it...that is when you sell yourself into slavery. **Our debt owed to sin and death was so great we could never afford it, so by default we were made slaves to it.**

But a kinsman redeemer (*Jesus Christ*) stepped in to pay our debt to sin and death and offer us freedom from that debt, but that makes us essentially slaves to Christ. But here's a better way to put it: we can continue in our slavery to sin and death for all eternity — sin and death are harsh masters — or we can be indebted to our loving Creator, who made our payment for us even though we don't deserve it, and thus voluntarily enter into servitude under Christ, our representative, whose "yoke is easy" and whose "burden is light" (Matthew 11:30).

---

1 This is a concise version by Bodie Hodge of the work produced by Bodie Hodge and Paul Taylor in the *New Answers Book 3*. Extra special thanks to Paul Taylor for his work in researching this.

2 Answers in Genesis opposes both racism and slavery. According to the Bible, there is only one race – the human race, where all people are descended from Adam and Eve.

3 Personal correspondence with Reverend Mathew Anderson, Ottumwa, IA, February 3, 2007.

Q11 Unicorns and the Bible...

YOU'VE GOT TO BE KIDDING!

Dr. Tommy Mitchell

You may have heard the Bible called a book of fairy tales because it mentions unicorns. However, the biblical unicorn was not the imaginary horse-like creature we think of today.

THE BIBLE

The Old Testament refers to unicorns in nine verses,[1] always in the context of familiar animals — peacocks and eagles, lambs and lions, bullocks and goats, donkeys and horses, dogs and calves. Biblical unicorns also behaved like ordinary animals. They skip like calves in Psalm 29:6. And Isaiah 34:7 says, "The unicorns shall come down with them, and the bullocks with the bulls."[2]

God told Job in Job 39:9–11 that the unicorn was very strong but could not be tamed by man to pull a plow. God said, "Will the unicorn be willing to serve thee?" and "Will he harrow [plow] the valleys?" and "Wilt thou trust him, because his strength is great?" God reminded Job (in chapters 38 and 39) of a variety of impressive animals (including the behemoth, an animal whose description fits a sauropod dinosaur) to show Job that God the Creator was far above man in power and strength. Job had to be familiar with all the animals on God's list for the illustration to make sense to him.

Since we know from the verses in Job that unicorns were strong and stubborn, we can see that a strong horn on such a powerful, independent-minded creature would be a good symbol for strength. Many of the verses referring to the unicorn therefore use it as a symbol for strength. For instance, Numbers 23:22 says, "God brought them out of Egypt; he hath as it were the strength of an unicorn."

There are other creatures in the world with only single horns. How about the rhinoceros and narwhal? The absence of a unicorn in the modern world should not cause us to doubt its past existence. So do we have any idea what the ancient unicorn looked like?

One-horned Rhino

The elasmotherium , an extinct giant rhinoceros, is a possibility. Its 33-inch-long skull has a huge bony protuberance on the front consistent with the supporting base of a massive horn.

Archaeologist Austen Henry Layard excavated the ruins of ancient Ninevah — the Assyrian city where Jonah preached. Layard sketched a single-horned creature from an Assyrian obelisk along with two-horned bovine animals; he thought the single-horned animal was an Indian rhinoceros.

Marco Polo described rhinoceros-like unicorns in Sumatra. He even wrote that those big hairy brutes were nothing like the legendary unicorns that could be tamed by gentle maidens! (*That mythological creature appeared in fanciful stories from North Africa around the second to fourth centuries.*)

Several ancient writers — the fourth century Greek physician/historian Ctesias as well as Aelian, Strabo, Pliny the Elder, and Tertullian — wrote about real unicorns, some mentioning, like the Book of Job, that they could not be domesticated. So the biblical unicorn could have been the elasmotherium. In fact, a margin note in the 1769 edition of the King James Version of the Bible suggests it.

WILD OX AND AUROCHS

The Hebrew word re'em, translated unicorn in many English translations as well as in the Bible in some other languages, resembles the Assyrian word for "wild ox," rimu. Therefore, some people think the unicorn was the two-horned aurochs. Fighting rimu was a popular sport for Assyrian kings.

Julius Caesar, the first Roman emperor, described the phenomenal size, shape, and unique appearance of this powerful creature's horns. The aurochs, extinct since 1627, had horns so symmetrical they could appear as one in profile. Assyrian obelisks and Indus River seals do depict apparent single-horned creatures, but some people interpret these as artistic symmetry and believe the two-horned aurochs was only called a unicorn because it looked like one from the side.

CONCLUSION

Whether the biblical unicorn was a one-horned creature like the elasmotherium or possibly the symmetrically horned aurochs, the strong horn serves as a symbol of great strength to the Bible reader.

The importance of the biblical unicorn is not so much its specific identity — much as we would like to know it — but its reality. **The Bible is clearly describing a real animal.**

The unicorn mentioned in the Bible was a powerful animal possessing one *(or potentially two strong horns)* — not the fantasy animal that has been popularized in legends and toys. Whatever it was, the unicorn is now likely extinct like many other animals. And this is a good point: just because something has gone extinct, doesn't mean it didn't exist! To think of the biblical unicorn as a fantasy animal is to demean God's Word, which is true in every detail.

---

1 Unicorns are mentioned in the following verses in the King James Bible as well as many other ancient translations: Job 39:9–12; Numbers 23:22; Numbers 24:8; Deuteronomy 33:17; Psalm 22:21; Psalm 29:6; Psalm 92:10; and Isaiah 34:7

2 All passages in this chapter are taken from the KJV.

Q12 How can we be sure the 66 books of the Bible are

THE ONLY ONES
FROM GOD ?

Bodie Hodge

Some people argue that when Christians say that all the books of the Bible are from God, they should not be able to use the Bible itself in their defense. But that is absurd! Think about it like this: can an army use a hill to help them defend that hill? Yes, they can! And we can use the Bible when defending the Bible!

So the Bible is not off limits when we talk about "canon." No, I'm not talking about what an army uses in war — that is a "cannon"! I'm talking about the "canon" that means the "standard" or the "measure" used to evaluate all things. In other words, it is the collection of Scriptures that are God's Word.

The word canon comes from the Greek word *kanon*, which referred to a reed that was used for measuring (*e.g., a standard measurement*). Our English word cane still reflects this Greek word.

The 66 books of the Bible — the canon — are the Word of God, inspired and inerrant in the original autographs. The Bible consists of books inspired by God, and written or affirmed by Jewish prophets (for the Old Testament) and by Apostles (*for the New Testament*).

71

Old Testament

The overall Jewish breakdown of the Old Testament books is in three major categories:[1]

1. The Law *(the Hebrew name is Torah)*: Genesis, Exodus, Leviticus, Numbers, and Deuteronomy

2. The Prophets *(the Hebrew name is Nebhim)*:

> 1. Early prophets: Joshua, Judges, Samuel, and Kings
>
> 2. Later prophets: Isaiah, Jeremiah, Ezekiel, and the Twelve *(Minor Prophets)*

3. The Psalms/Writings *(the Hebrew name is Kethubhim)*:

> 1. Poetic books: Psalms, Proverbs, and Job
>
> 2. Five Rolls: Songs of Songs, Ruth, Lamentations, Esther, and Ecclesiastes
>
> 3. Historical books: Daniel, Ezra-Nehemiah, and Chronicles

The Jewish canon includes exactly what was in the Protestant Bible and was what was used in the early churches. The number of books is different, but it is the same text. Where Protestants [and early Catholics] divided Kings, Samuel, and Chronicles into two books apiece, the Jews had them as one. The books of Ezra and Nehemiah were also compiled as one book in the Jewish list. The 12 minor prophets were also accumulated into one book.

Jesus confirms all three divisions in the Old Testament in Luke 24:44, showing that they were authoritative canon books.

Now He said to them, "These are My words which I spoke to you while I was still with you, that all things which are written about Me in the Law of Moses and the Prophets and the Psalms must be fulfilled" (Luke 24:44; NASB).

Even other New Testament authors openly confirmed the Old Testament. For example, Paul affirms them as oracles of God (Romans 3:1–2).

Old Testament books

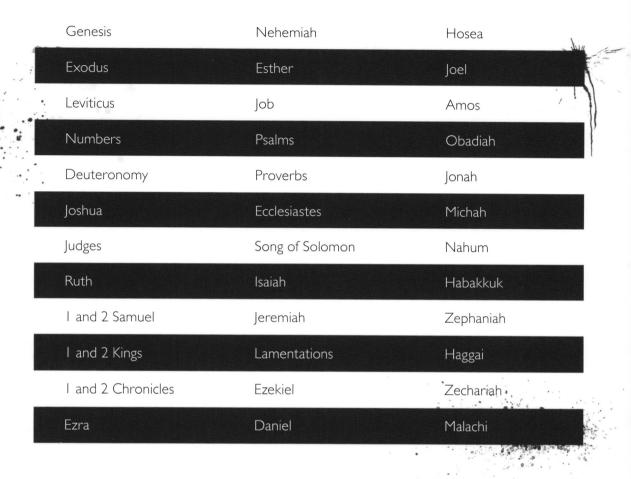

Genesis	Nehemiah	Hosea
Exodus	Esther	Joel
Leviticus	Job	Amos
Numbers	Psalms	Obadiah
Deuteronomy	Proverbs	Jonah
Joshua	Ecclesiastes	Michah
Judges	Song of Solomon	Nahum
Ruth	Isaiah	Habakkuk
1 and 2 Samuel	Jeremiah	Zephaniah
1 and 2 Kings	Lamentations	Haggai
1 and 2 Chronicles	Ezekiel	Zechariah
Ezra	Daniel	Malachi

New Testament

The New Testament books, having apostolic authority, are affirmed through Christ. The 27 books of the New Testament require some deeper thinking because they were written after Christ ascended, so some may think that we do not have His authority for them. **Did Christ give any hints that there would be more books of the Bible or hints as to how and by whom they may arrive? Absolutely!**

In John 14, Jesus is speaking with His disciples, who were Apostles. He claimed that the Holy Spirit would remind them of things that had happened.

But the Helper, the Holy Spirit, whom the Father will send in My name, He will teach you all things, and bring to your remembrance all that I said to you (John 14:26; NASB).

When the Helper comes, whom I will send to you from the Father, that is the Spirit of truth who proceeds from the Father, He will testify about Me, and you will testify also, because you have been with Me from the beginning (John 15:26–27; NASB).

Christ's statements "bring to your remembrance" and "you will testify also" shows that we should expect some teachings from the Apostles for future generations, perhaps in the form of letters, books, sermons, and so on. **In other words, Apostles were confirmed by Christ to be able to speak or affirm the very Word of God through the Holy Spirit.**

In the past, no prophets were able to do things on their own, but only as they were moved by the Holy Spirit (2 Peter 1:21). The same was true for the Apostles in the New Testament; they were able to do things as the Holy Spirit moved them. Furthermore, New Testament books have similar statements to those in the Old Testament claiming to be from God. For examples, see 1 Peter 1:12, 1 Corinthians 2:12–13, 1 Thessalonians 4:1–2, and Colossians 4:16–18.

However, there is no reason to assume all the Apostles were gifted to write something, and not all of them did. Even many prophets of the Old Testament have no written documents. And while we may not have writings from every Apostle, the Bible does tell us who all the Apostles were:

Simon Peter; **Andrew** *(Peter's brother)*; **James**, the son of Zebedee; **John**, the son of Zebedee and brother of James; **Philip**; **Bartholomew**; **Thomas**; **Matthew**, the tax collector, **James**, the son of Alphaeus; **Lebbaeus Thaddaeus**; **Simon**, the Canaanite; **Judas Iscariot**, who forfeited his right as an Apostle; **Matthias** (Acts 1:20-26), who replaced Judas; **Paul** (2 Corinthians 11:5, 2 Corinthians 12:11, etc.); **Barnabas** (Acts 14:14); **James**, the brother of Jesus (Galatians 1:19); **Jesus**, who is THE Apostle (Hebrews 3:1)

New Testament Books

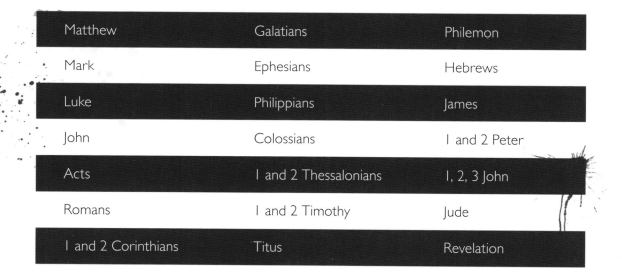

Matthew	Galatians	Philemon
Mark	Ephesians	Hebrews
Luke	Philippians	James
John	Colossians	1 and 2 Peter
Acts	1 and 2 Thessalonians	1, 2, 3 John
Romans	1 and 2 Timothy	Jude
1 and 2 Corinthians	Titus	Revelation

The Apostles, through the Holy Spirit and by the guidance of Christ, had the authority to write or approve books that are canon:

Therefore the wisdom of God also said, "I will send them prophets and apostles, and some of them they will kill and persecute" (Luke 11:49).

...having been built on the foundation of the apostles and prophets, Jesus Christ Himself being the chief cornerstone (Ephesians 2:20).

WHICH BOOKS ARE NOT AUTHORITATIVE?

Books that are not Scripture would include the Old or New Testament apocryphal books, the gnostic gospels, and the apocalyptic literature surrounding New Testament times. John's apocalypse, otherwise known as the Book of Revelation, is the only authoritative apocalyptic book in the New Testament as opposed to the plethora of 1st and 2nd century apocryphal writings that are not Scripture (*other biblical books may have apocalyptic sections though*).

From a biblical perspective, no other alleged writings are to be included in the canon of Scripture, as the canon was closed when the last Apostle, John, died in the first century. There are several writings that are not Scripture:

- **Decrees issued under papal authority**, which is observed in the Roman Church

- **Islam's Koran** (*Qu'ran*), hadith, or anything else claimed to come from Muhammad

- **Mormon writings** (*the Mormon institution is otherwise known as the Church of Jesus Christ of Latter Day Saints*) such as the *Book of Mormon, Pearl of Great Price, Doctrines and Covenants*, or any other writings by Mormon leaders or their founder Joseph Smith since the 1800s.

- **Jehovah's Witnesses' writings** such as the *Watchtower* publications (*e.g., the Watchtower magazine or the Awake magazine*), or Charles Taze Russell's (*founder of the Jehovah's Witnesses in the 1800s*) Studies in the Scriptures, or later Jehovah's Witnesses leaders' comments

- **Hindu wisdom books** such as the Vedas or Bhagavad Gita

- **All other claimed "holy" books**

Both Jehovah's Witnesses and Mormons have taken the Bible and changed its words in multiple places to conform to their theology, so be on the guard for these other "translations." The Jehovah's Witnesses use the New World Translation, and the Mormons use the King James Version of 1833 (*not to be confused with respectable versions of the KJV*). The Mormons also call this version the JST (*Joseph Smith Translation*).

Naturally, these other claimed holy books (*as well as many others*) **contradict the Holy Bible, and therefore cannot be from God, as God cannot contradict Himself.** Also keep in mind that each of these cults and religions has claims of people being prophets, like Muhammad, Joseph Smith, or the Watchtower organization.

The problem is that they came well after the time of the prophets and Apostles. The Lord conferred on the Apostles of Jesus Christ the final responsibility of the Scriptures above all prophets (1 Corinthians, 12:28). So when the last Apostle of Jesus Christ died, John, that ended the Scriptures.

Finally, Romans 3:1–2 indicates that the Jews were entrusted with the oracles of God. This is why the Old and New Testaments were written or affirmed[2] by Jews *(prophets or apostles)*. These others were not Jewish nor are they Apostles of Jesus Christ, so they cannot be from God.

CONCLUSION

We know the Bible is true based on internal evidence of the Bible itself *(confirmation comes from Old Testament prophets and New Testament Apostles alone)*, and authoritative Scripture is limited to the 66 books of the Bible. It was not decided upon at Nicea in A.D. 325, which some people mistakenly appeal to. God's Word was God's Word the moment it was written. The books of the Bible, made up of the Old *(39 books total)* and New Testaments *(27 books total)*, are the written Word of God.

The Bible is divinely inspired and inerrant throughout. Its assertions are factually true in all the original autographs. It is the supreme authority in everything it teaches. Its authority is not limited to spiritual, religious, or redemptive themes, but also includes its assertions in such fields as history and science.

1 Josh McDowell, A Ready Defense *(Nashville, TN: Thomas Nelson Publishers, 1993)*, p. 35.

2 For example, according to the church fathers, Luke's Gospel was a record of Paul's sermons and affirmed by Paul, a Jew. In the same fashion, Mark was affirmed by Peter. Peter and Paul were both Jews and Apostles.

What about

ABORTION, CLONING, AND STEM CELLS?

At school I'm taught that these things are good for society!

Dr. Tommy Mitchell

Have you ever wondered about abortion? Whether it is right or wrong to have one? You may have heard things like, "A woman has a right over her own body." The law says abortion is legal, but does that mean it's right? And what is the big deal about similar topics like stem cells and cloning?

How Do We Know Whether Abortion Is Right or Wrong?

Abortion refers to killing a baby before it is born. While people do have a right to make many decisions about their own bodies, the decision to abort a baby pits the rights of a pregnant woman against her unborn baby's right to life. Most people realize killing a baby is wrong. According to God's Word, killing an innocent person is murder (Proverbs 6:16–17). Because God created people with a conscience, even people who do not trust God's Word understand that murder is wrong (Romans 2:15).

So if killing a newborn baby is wrong, wouldn't it still be wrong to kill a baby the day before it is born? What about a month before it is born? Of course, that would still be murder. Some people say it is okay to kill a baby if it isn't mature enough to survive outside its mother's womb. The trouble is, babies a little too young to survive outside the womb still look like babies. Babies are supposed to be born after about nine months in the mother's body. And the age at which a baby can survive with medical care gets younger and younger. **So are some abortions okay and others not?** Where should people draw the line?

Unborn Babies Aren't Really Babies, Are They?

A baby's life begins when a sperm fertilizes an egg. You have heard that your chromosomes carry the blueprint — the complete instructions — for your human characteristics. Once fertilization happens, the zygote that is formed has a complete blueprint as a human being. A zygote doesn't look human, but if it survives and grows, it will soon look like the tiny baby it is. In fact, the zygote is already either a boy or a girl. Just a few days after fertilization, the zygote has changed names a couple of times and grown larger. Then it attaches to the wall of the mother's womb for nourishment, and the tiny baby grows there for nine months.

Some people think it is okay to abort a baby if doesn't look like a baby yet. But this is just their mere opinion. **Consider that a developing baby has a beating heart just four weeks after fertilization, fully formed fingers and toes just two weeks after that, and a week later is sucking his or her thumb.** If it looks like a baby and moves like a baby and even hiccups like a baby, isn't it a baby?

The information that makes up a new person is present at fertilization and it is a new combination of information, so right from the start the baby is a unique individual. God says in Psalm 139:16 that He sees an unborn baby even while he or she is "yet unformed." God knows a baby is a baby even before he or she looks like a baby.

A person's life begins at fertilization and continues through many stages, so when is it okay to murder a baby? Never. After all, you wouldn't think it was okay to kill a child just because she hadn't reached the stage of being able to walk. So why would anyone think it is okay to kill a baby just because she hasn't fully acquired her baby shape?

Many people who aren't comfortable with the idea of abortion change their tune when a pregnancy inconveniences their lives. **But murder doesn't become okay just because the alternative is inconvenient.**

What's the Big Deal About Embryonic Stem Cells?

Embryo is the word used to refer to a developing baby for the first eight weeks of life. Uninjured and properly nourished, a human embryo will continue to grow and develop until born and continues growing and changing all through childhood. But some people think it is okay to kill a tiny embryo in order to harvest its cells for experiments. They hope those experiments will someday provide cures for some diseases.

But would it be okay to murder a baby to cure another person's disease?
Of course not. So why would anyone think it is okay to murder a very small baby? Many say the embryo is not a baby, just a blob of cells. But as we've already seen, the complete human blueprint is in that embryo, and the embryo is already progressing steadily toward the time it will kick, cry, walk, and talk. What difference does it make if the embryo has not yet acquired a human "look"? Remember, God sees the baby when he or she is "yet unformed"!

Perhaps you've wondered where these embryos come from. You've heard of "test tube babies" — babies whose lives begin with fertilization of an egg by a sperm in a laboratory. Although the baby's life begins in the laboratory, after a few days the embryo is placed in its human mother to finish developing. If there are extra embryos, they can actually be frozen — sort of like the science fiction idea of "suspended animation." That way they can be saved and placed into a mother's body to finish developing later.

All the embryos formed in the laboratory from the same mother and father are brothers and sisters of each other. But if there are more embryos than people want, the "extras" are often destroyed to get their stem cells for research. Most people would never think of destroying their own children. **But isn't destroying extra embryos the same thing?**

By taking a position against embryonic stem cell research, Christians are often accused of standing against medical progress. Some people claim being against embryonic stem cell research means we don't care about sick people! Nothing could be further from the truth.

I spent over 20 years practicing medicine. I loved and cared for my patients each and every day and welcomed new cures. I took a solemn oath to care for the sick but to "first, do no harm." And murdering a person to save another is definitely "harm"!

So If We Reject Embryonic Stem Cell Research, Then What?

The alternative is adult stem cells. These cells are obtained from mature tissues. No destruction of an embryo is required. There has been much progress in medical research using adult stem cells, and many clinical trials using these treatments on real patients are going on right now.

Then there is the question of clones. A clone is a copy. No one has succeeded in making a clone of a human being — yet. But scientists have made clones of animals. The first mammal to be cloned in the laboratory was named Dolly. She was a sheep. Dolly's life started in the laboratory, sort of like test tube babies do, but without the usual fertilization process. Scientists figured out how to clone — or copy — a sheep cell to grow a whole new sheep. Some scientists would like to figure out how to clone people, too.

Research to clone humans is done with the idea of making cloned embryos for research, not with the intention of growing extra children. **In other words, their lives are started in the laboratory with the intention of killing them.** If having a baby just so you can kill him for his parts is wrong — and it would be — then cloning a person for parts is just as wrong.

We keep saying murder is wrong. Why? What's the difference between killing a child and killing a cow? Well, people are not animals. About 6,000 years ago, God made many kinds of plants and animals. And He also made Adam and Eve, the first human beings. Only Adam and Eve were made in the image of God. As such they — and we — are not only able to think and reason and communicate in ways no animal can but also to understand and communicate with our Creator.

All human beings — regardless of their age or even their disabilities — have souls that will live forever — souls that God cares about. God created the entire universe, but He says that each and every human being is His own special creation whom He "fearfully and wonderfully" (Psalm 139:14) knit together in the womb for the purpose of glorifying Himself. God sent His Son Jesus Christ to die, according to Hebrews 2:9, in order to purchase salvation for each and every person.

God said that murdering human beings is evil and is sin. Killing a person is not the same thing as killing an animal because people are made in the image of God. Murder is always wrong according to Genesis 9:6. Murder is wrong whether the victim is an older person or a young child or a baby...even in the womb. Murder is just as wrong the day or month before a baby leaves the protection of his mother's womb. And if that "kind of murder" is wrong, then so is intentionally killing a baby many months before he should be able to live outside the womb. Murder is murder, no matter what you call it.

BUT WHAT IF...IT'S "TOO LATE!"

What if someone you know has had an abortion? What if you have had an abortion? Maybe it was somebody else's idea. Maybe you were scared and it was your own idea. Perhaps you didn't even realize how wrong you were. Now you know the truth.

But you need to know an even more powerful and more important truth.
Just like everybody else, you are a sinner, but you are sinner that Jesus Christ the Son of God loves. Jesus came into this world as a little baby and grew to be a man so He could die on the Cross for your sins and mine.

The day He died on that Cross, He knew that someday you would be born and need His shed blood to cover your guilt. He even knew the sins you would commit. He even knew about the abortion. And right now, He wants you to repent of that sin and of all your sin. He wants you to trust Him and to know that when He died on the Cross, **He was dying for you to cover that sin.**

Jesus didn't stay dead. He rose from the dead, showing that He has power over life and death, and we expect that since Jesus is the Creator (John1, Colossians 1, and Hebrews 1). He did that to give you a brand new life. He wants you to know that He loves you and He forgives you.

Tell Him you're sorry for all your sins and ask Him to forgive you. He promises He will. First John 1:9 says, "If we confess our sins, He is faithful and just to forgive us our sins and to cleanse us from all unrighteousness." When you know Jesus has forgiven you, you know He has given you a brand new life. I hope you love Him and will follow Him always.

83

What about going

TO COLLEGE?

Ken Ham

Are there any solid Christian colleges left that believe in biblical authority? I mean, so many of them teach non-Christian views nowadays...

Choosing a college to receive your undergraduate and graduate training is a very important decision that will affect the rest of your life in many ways.

A friend of mine once said, "If you find the perfect church, don't join it or you will ruin it!" Well, I can also adapt that for college: "If you find the perfect college, don't go there or you will ruin it."

My point is that there is no perfect Christian college, seminary, or Bible college. We live in a fallen world. Having said that, there are definitely those schools that are more "fallen" than others!

Before I give my counsel in regard to this complex question, let me say first of all that ultimately the decision you make as to which college you attend is between you, your parents, and the Lord. I would presume that Christians would bathe their decisions in prayer, and then be responsible in checking out each potential college with diligent research. In regard to a Christian college, Christians need to carefully investigate what it teaches, the college's stand on the authority of Scripture, how the curriculum and faculty develop your Christian worldview, and so on.

Anyway, here is my counsel based on years of experience and my understanding of Scripture as applied to this topic.

Secular Colleges and Universities

It is important to understand that there is no neutrality in regard to one's worldview. The Bible states that we walk either in light or in darkness. Matthew 12:30 states, "He who is not with Me is against Me, and he who does not gather with Me scatters abroad."

Knowing that, we need to be upfront and recognize that secular colleges are certainly not for Christ, so they must be against! The starting point that most of the professors will stand on (e.g., *that there is no God, or God has nothing to do with their worldview*) will determine the nature of the philosophy in which they will try to indoctrinate you. So you need to be on your guard.

If you choose to go to a secular college, make sure you are prepared with the resources you will need to study to maintain an unpolluted worldview. There is no doubt that some exceptional Christian students have started college already prepared theologically and scientifically to defend their faith so they can be a witness at such institutions.

But — beware! The anti-Christian sentiment is growing rapidly in the USA *(and our Western world in general)*, and we are seeing more and more instances of professors persecuting those they know to be Christians. Sometimes they might even disallow Christians into certain programs, or not let them obtain higher degrees.

Personally, I would try to avoid attending a secular college if at all possible. My first choice would be to attend a Bible-believing Christian college. However, I do understand that some programs aren't available at Christian colleges — and there are not that many Christian colleges I would even recommend for consideration.

However, if you are going to go to a secular college — here is my advice:

1. **If at all possible, do not live in the dorms.** The best option would be to live with your parents — but at the very least, try to live off campus with some other dedicated Christians.

2. **Check out the Christian groups on campus.** Keep in mind that many compromise with evolution and/or millions of years — so be careful. Continue to diligently study God's Word. And bathe your time in prayer.

3. **Be sensitive to the fact that there are faculty who will do their best to dissuade you from being a Christian.** And if you are (*and I trust you are*) a six-day, young earth creationist — in most instances it is probably best to be a "closet" creationist. There is an increasing anti-creationist sentiment amongst faculty at such colleges.

4. **Make sure you continue to study resources from Answers in Genesis and other solid apologetics resources to help you avoid becoming contaminated by secular philosophy.** Subscribe to *Answers* magazine, and check out Answers in Genesis's website regularly for articles to help you answer skeptical questions and to help ward off doubts that may arise because of what you are taught in a secular school environment.

CHRISTIAN COLLEGES AND UNIVERSITIES

I would encourage you, if at all possible, to choose a Bible-believing Christian college for your studies. However, this is where there is a massive problem. Yes, there are hundreds of colleges that would claim they are "Christian" — but what do they mean by that word?

In 2011, the president of a Christian university and I wrote a book called *Already Compromised*. In that book, we detailed research that was conducted by America's Research Group into what Christian colleges teach, particularly in regard to the Book of Genesis. The results of the research showed the majority of professors would teach millions of years and evolutionary ideas.

It is important to understand that whether one believes in millions of years or evolutionary ideas is not a salvation issue as such (*salvation is conditioned upon faith in Christ — Christ alone*), but it is an authority issue. Sadly, I have met many young people over the years who went to a Christian college as zealous Christians, only to have their faith undermined by what they were taught. They succumbed to doubts as to whether they could really trust the Bible because of the teaching of evolution and/or millions of years, and they walked away from the Lord. I wouldn't want that to happen to any of you.

In fact, I would say that in many ways it would be worse for a Christian to attend a compromising Christian college than to go to a secular college. At least you would go (*hopefully*) knowing that a secular college will teach from a secular worldview. However, Christian colleges that compromise teach students as if this compromise is totally Christian — and this causes many students to succumb to doubt and ultimately unbelief — just like Adam and Eve when they were tempted with "Did God really say...? (Genesis 3:1).

CONCLUSION

I want you to consider this verse of Scripture:

You are the salt of the earth; but if the salt loses its flavor, how shall it be seasoned? It is then good for nothing but to be thrown out and trampled underfoot by men (Matthew 5:13).

Salt loses its saltiness when it is contaminated! Contamination destroys. It is so important for Christians, as the salt of the earth, to avoid as much contamination as possible.

The bottom line: I would recommend you consider a Bible-believing Christian college that does its best to avoid "contamination" — a college that will try to honor God's Word and not knowingly compromise God's Word in any way.

There is no perfect college that will do this. Even the best of colleges will have some deficiencies, or some faculty who may believe or teach something they shouldn't. So make sure you prepare yourself in the same way I recommended you prepare yourself for a secular college — keeping up today with Answers in Genesis and other apologetics resources, studying God's Word, prayer, and so forth.

However, to help you, *Answers in Genesis* has developed this special website:

www.creationcolleges.org

The colleges listed on this website have to sign a statement that they support/agree with the statement of faith adhered to by *Answers in Genesis*.[1] Of course, they can't guarantee every professor and every textbook will adhere to that statement of faith. But this list at least narrows the field for you and is a starting point as you consider attending a God-honoring Christian college. And take the warning the apostle Paul gave Timothy to heart:

O Timothy! Guard what was committed to your trust, avoiding the profane and idle babblings and contradictions of what is falsely called knowledge — by professing it some have strayed concerning the faith. Grace be with you. Amen (1 Timothy 6:20–21).

---

[1] Answers in Genesis Statement of Faith can be found here: http://www.answersingenesis.org/about/faith.

"Going Through the Motions"...

IS THAT SAVING FAITH?

Bodie Hodge

I want to talk about something very important. But let's see if you can spot it first. What is wrong with this short conversation?

"Hey Andy, have you received the risen Christ as your Lord and Savior?"

"John, you know I go to church, so of course I'm a Christian."

Did you catch it? Andy didn't really answer the question, did he? And this is a key point: just because someone calls himself a Christian or goes to church doesn't really mean he is saved.

Now don't get me wrong — sometimes a person like this is a genuine believer and simply doesn't realize that he failed to answer the question. It may be good to clarify and ask again even more directly. But other times, people who call themselves "Christians" do so for reasons that are not biblical, such as going to church. They do all the things Christians should, but they do not have faith in Christ. I call this "going through the motions" of Christianity. I had a conversation like the one above years ago, and it made me think about why I call myself a Christian.

I Surprised an Evangelist!

One day during my university years, a Christian from Sweden came up to me and saw that I was wearing a cross. **He asked me, "Do you know what that cross means?"**

I answered something to the effect of "It represents the cross that Jesus Christ died on, and Christians often wear them as a reminder of that hope in Christ."

He then asked, "Are you a Christian?"

I said, "Yes."

Then he asked me something that I initially thought seemed a little redundant: *"Do you believe in Jesus Christ as your Lord and Savior, and do you believe He was raised from the dead?"*

The man's question was insightful, because he didn't assume that when someone said they were a "Christian," they had a saving belief in Jesus Christ. I answered, "Yes, I believe Jesus died and rose again to cover my sin and to save me, and I believe in Him as my Lord and Savior."

In one sense, I think he was shocked. He was probably not used to getting that answer from most of the people at this very secular university! But I remember thinking that he had great tact in witnessing. Not only was he kind and respectful toward me, which is how people sharing the gospel should act, but he also didn't take for granted that someone who said they were a "Christian" really was. He wanted to find out if I really believed in the Lord Jesus, or if I was simply "going through the motions." I have tremendous respect for that evangelist, and I hope that others would follow his example and not be afraid to stand up and witness about Jesus Christ in the same way he did.

REFLECTING ON WHAT IT REALLY MEANS TO BE A CHRISTIAN

Over the years, I realized what he meant. Salvation comes by faith in Jesus Christ, not by attending church (though it is important to attend a church), having Christian parents, or living in a "Christian nation." There are many people who say they are Christians for these and other reasons, but that doesn't mean they have faith in Christ. They might call themselves "Christians" because their parents are. I knew someone who was an atheist and has now become a universe-worshiping "spiritist" who describes himself as a pagan but also called himself a "Christian" because his parents were!

Sometimes people call themselves "Christians" because of their cultural background. For example, in Europe, many atheists still call themselves "Christians" because of the Christian heritage of Europe. But probably the most common reason is that many people who only go through the motions of Christianity (like sitting through church, going to youth groups and Christian events, and so on) may never have received Jesus Christ as their Lord and may not really believe it in their hearts.

One poll of professing evangelical Christians revealed that 27 percent of people in an evangelical church do NOT believe in absolute truth.[1] **Now consider this: God is the absolute truth! The Bible is the absolute truth!** Yet people sitting in pews and going to church are not convinced of absolute truth, and therefore they are not convinced of God and His truth in Scripture!

I hope you are not like this. But if you are, I want to challenge you to rethink what you believe. Here are some great passages you should consider. Romans 10:17 says, "So then faith comes by hearing, and hearing by the word of God."

93

THE GENESIS-ROMANS ROAD TO SALVATION

Genesis 1:1 — [God made everything.]

In the beginning God created the heavens and the earth.

Genesis 1:31 — [God made everything perfectly — no death, no suffering].

Then God saw everything that He had made, and indeed it was very good. So the evening and the morning were the sixth day.

Genesis 3:17–19 — [The punishment for sin is death, and because of sin the world is no longer perfect.]

Romans 5:12 — [Because Adam, our mutual grandfather, sinned, we now sin, too.]

Therefore, just as through one man sin entered the world, and death through sin, and thus death spread to all men, because all sinned.

Romans 3:23 — [We need to realize that we are all sinners, including ourselves.]

For all have sinned and fall short of the glory of God.

Romans 6:23 — [The punishment for sin is a just punishment — death — but God came to rescue us and give the free gift of salvation by sending His son Jesus.]

For the wages of sin is death, but the gift of God is eternal life in Christ Jesus our Lord.

Romans 10:9 – [To receive this free gift of salvation, you need to believe in Jesus as your risen Lord and Savior. Salvation is not by works, but by faith — see also John 3:16 and Acts 16:30–31.]

That if you confess with your mouth the Lord Jesus and believe in your heart that God has raised Him from the dead, you will be saved.

Romans 5:1 — [Being saved, you are now justified and have peace with God.]

Therefore, having been justified by faith, we have peace with God through our Lord Jesus Christ.

ENCOURAGEMENT

Our hope is that you truly give your life to Christ. We want to see people saved from this sin-cursed, death-ridden, and broken world. It would be a shame to go through the motions all your life but never really receive God's free gift of salvation. The Bible says:

For what will it profit a man if he gains the whole world, and loses his own soul? (Mark 8:36).

"Going through the motions" is not faith; it is works, so it cannot save you. You need Jesus Christ, the Son of God, who paid on the Cross the infinite punishment that you *(and all the rest of us)* deserve. Only God the Son, who is infinite, could take the infinite punishment from the infinite God the Father to make salvation possible. We, as mankind in Adam, messed up God's perfect world, and Christ, in His love, stepped in to save us (Romans 5:8). **He is a truly loving God.**

But as many as received Him, to them He gave the right to become children of God, to those who believe in His name (John 1:12).

I Carl Kerby, "WDJS, not just WWJD," *Answers in Genesis*, May 11, 2000, http://www.answersingenesis.org/articles/2000/05/11/wdjs-wwjd, accessed March 25, 2012.

Great Books for Teens!

1. *Answers Books for Teens (all volumes)* by Bodie Hodge, Tommy Mitchell, and Ken Ham — These books answer many of the questions teens ask most regarding the creation/evolution debate and how we know the Bible is true.

2. *Begin*, edited by Ken Ham and Bodie Hodge — This is a great starting point for teens. It takes you through the big picture of the Bible and connects the history using Genesis 1–11, the Ten Commandments, Book of John, Book of Romans, and the last two chapters of Revelation. There are comments to help you through the text with fascinating facts and some basics at the end.

3. *The Great Dinosaur Mystery Solved!* by Ken Ham — This book will help you understand dinosaurs from a biblical perspective.

4. *The Fall of Satan* by Bodie Hodge — This book answers many questions surrounding the fall of Satan and the Fall of mankind in the Garden of Eden. It looks at the issue of evil and gives a powerful presentation of the gospel.

5. *How Could a Loving God...?* by Ken Ham — A powerful book that looks at why the world is full of death and suffering.

6. *Dragons: Legends and Lore of Dinosaurs* by Bodie Hodge and Laura Welch — This book explores the connection between dragons of history and dinosaurs. It is fully illustrated and great for the whole family.

7. *Demolishing Supposed Bible Contradictions (2 volumes)*, edited by Ken Ham, Bodie Hodge, and Tim Chaffey — These books demolish the attack that the Bible is full of alleged contradictions. The books are composed of easy-to-understand short responses by a variety of authors to the most common contradictions.

8. *Evolution Exposed: Biology and Evolution Exposed: Earth Science* by Roger Patterson — These two books analyze the secular biology and earth science textbooks that are used in most public/state schools (and even in some Christian schools) and identify where evolution and millions of years crop up (*sometimes it is very subtle!*). They also show you how to refute these false claims.

9. *A Pocket Guide to...series* — This series is made up of a number of short books. Each discuss a particular topic, like dinosaurs, global warming, a young earth, Noah's Ark, ape-men, the global Flood, and many more.

10. *Already Compromised* by Ken Ham — If you're looking for a good Christian college to attend, this book is a must read!

Where Can I Get These?

All these books can be purchased through Answers in Genesis at **www.answersingenesis.org** or by calling 800-778-3390.

Most of these books can also be purchased through New Leaf Press/Master Books at **nlpg.com/masterbooks** or by calling 800-999-3777.